The Gospel of Mark

Question by Question

The Gospel of Mark

Question by Question

Timothy R. Carmody

Paulist Press
New York/Mahwah, NJ

Cover and book design by Lynn Else

Library of Congress Cataloging-in-Publication Data

Carmody, Timothy R.
    The Gospel of Mark / Timothy R. Carmody.
        p. cm. — (Question by question)
    Includes bibliographical references (p.   ).
    ISBN 978-0-8091-4636-9 (alk. paper)
    1. Bible. N.T. Mark—Textbooks. I. Title.
    BS2586.C36 2010
    226.3'07—dc22

                                                                2009041055

Published by Paulist Press
997 Macarthur Boulevard
Mahwah, New Jersey 07430

www.paulistpress.com

Printed and bound in the
United States of America

Contents

Contents

In loving memory of my parents,
Raphael and Dorothy Carmody

General Introduction

During the past century, a consensus has emerged in biblical studies regarding the relationship between the three Synoptic Gospels (Matthew, Mark, and Luke). Previously, the tradition held that Matthew was the first Gospel written and served as the source for both the Gospel of Mark and the Gospel of Luke. With the advent of historical criticism, scholars recognized that Mark was the earliest of the Gospels and that Matthew and Luke both used Mark as a source. The reasons for this belief are that Mark is the shortest of the three; it has the poorest and most awkward Greek; Mark's language often contains remnants of Aramaic phraseology and grammar; and Mark has the lowest Christology (picture of the divinity of Christ). These facts do not prove that Mark is the earliest Gospel, but taken together they make a good case that it is.

There is no consensus about the date of Mark, but it is generally agreed that it was written sometime between 60 and 75 CE. There are a variety of opinions about where the Gospel was written. The tradition of the earliest Christian writers maintained that the Gospel was written in Rome, and many scholars still believe Rome is the most plausible location. However, other scholars have argued for a Syrian or North Palestinian provenance for the book, and still others for a provenance in Alexandria.

The Gospel clearly indicates that the community has undergone, or is undergoing, some sort of persecution, which would fit well with Nero's persecution of Christians in Rome in 62–64 CE. Jesus in Mark's Gospel also speaks of a wife divorcing her husband (10:12). A wife having the legal standing to divorce her husband would only have been allowed under Roman law in Rome or a Roman city.

The author of the Gospel of Mark is unknown. The Gospel has traditionally been attributed to a writer named Mark. It was commonly thought that the Mark of this Gospel was John Mark,

1

mentioned in the Acts of the Apostles as a companion of Barnabas and Paul (Acts 12:25). For our Bible study, the question of the historical Mark is not a concern. In this study, when we refer to "Mark" we are referring to the author of the Gospel of Mark, whoever that might be.

Two of the most distinctive organizing principles in the Gospel of Mark are repetition and framing. Mark will repeat an idea or experience many times in many different stories. Most of this repetition is Mark's own literary creation to make a theological point. The two most discussed repetitions in the Gospel of Mark are the repetition of the "Messianic Secret" and the "Failure of the Disciples." In numerous stories in Mark, Jesus tells those who are healed, the demons he casts out, and his disciples not to say anything about what has happened. This repetition of a narrative feature in the different stories has come to be known as the "Messianic Secret." Another repeated narrative feature that stands out in the Gospel of Mark is the repetition by the narrator and by Jesus of a negative evaluation of the disciples' understanding of Jesus' mission. This culminates in Jesus' closest disciples betraying him, denying him, and fleeing at his arrest.

A second characteristic of the Gospel of Mark is the use of stories that, in their repetition, provide a structure or frame into which other stories in the narrative fit. Mark repeats Jesus' prediction of his passion three times. This threefold repetition structures a whole collection of stories that are sandwiched between these predictions. There are other stories that are repeated just twice to form a frame around a section of material. Mark will use one story at the beginning of a block of material and a similar story at the end. The two stories about the multiplication of loaves, the sending out of the disciples and their return, the cursing of the fig tree and its withering, and the two cures of blind men are all good examples of this kind of structuring.

Some have divided Mark by the content—miracles in the first half and teaching on discipleship in the second, or by characters—crowds, disciples, and religious leaders. Certainly the natural flow of the narrative does not fit neatly into the chapter divisions (which were only added to the Gospel in the sixteenth century). In this study of the Gospel of Mark, I have chosen to divide the

Gospel into sections for study using the structuring elements discussed above.

Structural Outline of the Gospel of Mark

1:1–13	Introduction of Jesus and His Ministry
1:14—3:35	Beginning of Jesus' Ministry
4:1–34	Parable Chapter
4:35—6:6	Mighty Deeds
6:7–33	Meaning of Mission
6:34—8:21	Feeding Cycle
8:22—10:52	Passion Prediction Cycle
11:1—12:44	Debates in Jerusalem
13:1–37	Discourse on the Temple and the End Times
14:1–42	Events Leading to the Arrest
14:43—15:47	Trial and Crucifixion
16:1–20	Empty Tomb (and Resurrection Appearance)

Since the canonical Gospel of Mark ends at 16:20, we have included all of these verses in our discussion. It is universally agreed that Mark 16:9–20 (called the "longer ending") was a later addition to the original Gospel of Mark and is almost certainly dependent on the Gospels of Matthew and Luke for its version of the resurrection appearances of Jesus. Some have contended that the original ending of Mark has been lost, while many others believe that Mark 16:8 was the original ending of the Gospel.

"How to Use"
Reading Guide for Individual and Study Groups

This book may be read both individually and for group use as a way to study the Gospel of Mark. It is especially designed for adult Bible study groups to use over the course of several weeks with twelve sections encompassing the sixteen chapters of this Gospel.

The following may be helpful ways to make use of this book:

1. A study group should attend to the practical details as to frequency of meetings, when and where they will take place, length of time for each session, and how many sections per meeting will work well for the group.

2. It would be easier if the same English translation of the Bible is used by all group participants. *NAB* (*New American Bible*) version is generally used by Roman Catholics and is the translation familiar to most because of its liturgical use. *NRSV* (*New Revised Standard Version*) is often cited by scholars and is used for the quotations in this text. There is a Catholic edition of the NRSV. Using the same text is a helpful basis for common reading, reflection, and discussion.

3. A group meeting should include reading aloud Scripture passages, praying in common, and discussing ways for practical applications of the Bible to daily life. The Introduction, Questions, and Conclusion in each section of this book are primarily designed for this purpose.

4. In reading and praying with the text, the group should pay attention to the personal reactions and responses to the story and the characters. These "reader reactions" will provide clues to the theological agenda of the evangelist. When

a reader says that the text made one feel a certain way, the next question should be, "What in the text caused the reader to have this reaction?" and then, "Why did the author want the reader to have this reaction?" "What theological point should the reader get from reacting to the text this way?"

5. Decide on how group leadership will operate. Will one individual be responsible as a group leader for preparing each session, or will the leadership rotate from session to session? The one leading the group needs to prepare prior to the meeting session.

6. Referring to the Answers Section after group members have shared their own personal responses will probably work best. It might be helpful to read them over, see what they offer in response to what the group response has been, and return to reviewing them the following week.

7. This book is not an academic textbook but a study guide of eighty-three different questions to help individuals and groups who use it to learn more about the Gospel of Mark, engage in a personal dialogue of their own experience of faith and to grow spiritually as twenty-first-century disciples of Jesus Christ.

8. The methodology favored in this text is a "close reading" of the narrative. It will be helpful for the group in using this particular book to be sensitive not just to "what" the evangelist writes, but "how" the evangelist tells the story. Much of the theology of Mark, the good news, is found in how he tells the story and not simply in the facts of the story. The group should pay attention to the literary context of each story, the plot, repeated words, themes, imagery, characterization, and narrator point of view. By paying close attention to how Mark tells the story you will gain much greater insight into what Mark wants the reader to experience and learn from the story.

9. The study of Scripture is very rewarding. Contemporary analyses and insights from biblical scholarship may be troubling and confusing to some since previous understandings and beliefs may be challenged. However as St. Jerome, who is responsible for translating the Bible into the Latin Vulgate edition, noted: *"Not knowing the Scriptures is to be ignorant of Christ."*

Questions

Section 1:
Mark 1:1–13

Introduction

The Gospel of Mark begins with what is often considered a title for the book: "The beginning of the good news of Jesus Christ, the Son of God" (1:1). This title contains the words *good news* or "gospel." *Gospel* was a word used for the proclamations of the great deeds of the emperor on behalf of the empire. Paul is the first to use the word for the proclamation of what God has done in Jesus Christ. The title of the book also contains two important titles of Jesus—Christ and Son of God. These titles set the tone and the agenda for the Gospel proclamation of who Jesus is and what his mission will be.

The narrative of the Gospel begins with a reference to what was written in the words of the prophets. This is a signal to the reader to read the whole story in reference to the scriptures—the law and the prophets. The Gospel writer's account of the story of Jesus Christ (Messiah) depends on typology and fulfillment. Imagine the Gospel writer painting his picture of Jesus on a blank canvas. There are no catechisms, no councils, and no dogmas. There are no bishops or seminaries. What are Christians supposed to believe about Jesus, his relationship to God, and his mission? The Gospel writer uses the images and words of the Old Testament that are familiar to his hearers and readers. The title, "Christ," is an Old Testament image that describes Jesus as the anointed king, chosen by God to save and lead God's people.

The cross-references contained in most study Bibles are an essential tool for reading and understanding the Gospels. If your Bible does not have them, you should invest in a Bible that does! When looking for cross-references to a story in Mark, it is often helpful to check the cross-references for the same story in Matthew. Because Matthew occurs first in the Bible, often the cross-references for that Gospel will be more complete. The authors of all the Gospels portray Jesus using Old Testament typology. The stories about the great figures of the Old Testament are the models or types for what Jesus does and who he is. Jesus is of the type of Moses or David or Elijah. The events of Jesus' life are of the type of the exodus or the exile. By using language that calls to mind these characters and events of the Old Testament, Mark paints for us a word picture of Jesus.

Mark describes Jesus as having the same qualities, mission, or relationship with God as these Old Testament heroes, or describes God as doing the same work in Jesus' life as God did in these Old Testament events. The Gospel writers will also use God as a type. At times, Jesus does what God has done or is expected to do in the Old Testament. For a modern reader it is usually necessary to have notes that lead the reader to the biblical texts behind these allusions. For many of the original audience, these allusions would have been easily recognizable.

This section is divided into three scenes, each one containing Old Testament typology. Each of the three scenes mentions the Holy Spirit. The Spirit descends on Jesus at his baptism, John the Baptist foretells that Jesus will baptize with the Holy Spirit, and it is the Spirit who drives Jesus into the desert to be tested. Jesus' ministry is entirely driven by the Spirit of God.

In the first scene, Mark quotes Malachi 3:1 about a messenger to come before the coming of God. Later in Malachi 4:5, this messenger is identified with Elijah. In Mark, this messenger is John the Baptist, who later in this same scene is dressed in the camel hair of Elijah (2 Kgs 1:18). Mark wants us to see John the Baptist as the type of Elijah, who is expected to return to prepare for the coming of God. Part of Mark's quotation is also from the prophet Isaiah whom Mark credits with the whole quotation. The words of Isaiah are taken from chapter 40, which promises a return from exile that is meant also to remind the reader of a new exodus. We can see that Mark wants the reader to understand that the salvation by God in Jesus will be a new exodus, a return from exile.

In the second scene the voice from heaven makes allusions to three Old Testament figures. In calling Jesus "son," the voice from heaven recalls the words of Psalm 2, in which God claims David as his son at David's coronation. By referring to Jesus as "beloved" son, the voice from heaven recalls the words of God to Abraham in reference to Abraham's beloved son, Isaac. And finally, the voice from heaven notes that in Jesus "I am well pleased," recalling God's words to his servant in Isaiah 42:1. It is only by knowing these allusions in the words of the voice from heaven that we can know what the voice of God is telling us, the reader, about who Jesus is.

The third scene, the testing in the desert, reminds the reader of the forty years the Hebrews wandered in the desert and were tested. It also reminds us of Elijah's forty days in the desert, a time when he was ministered to by angels (1 Kgs 19:5–8).

Questions

1. What is the author trying to tell the reader with the combined quotation from Malachi and Isaiah that is used to introduce John the Baptist?

2. To interpret the words of the voice from heaven at Jesus' baptism, read Genesis 22, Psalm 2, and Isaiah 42. Can you see that the words of the voice from heaven were created out of these Old Testament texts? What is Mark trying to tell the reader about who Jesus is by combining these allusions? What kind of Messiah is a blend of David, Isaac, and the suffering servant?

3. The story of Satan testing Jesus draws a comparison between the testing of Jesus and the testing of the Hebrews for forty years in the desert and the testing of Elijah for forty days (1 Kgs 19). What do these allusions tell us about the nature of Jesus' testing and the purpose of Jesus' ministry?

Conclusions

If Mark states right from the beginning who Jesus is, why does he need the rest of the Gospel? It is clear from Mark's Gospel that the Old Testament titles used for Jesus (Son of God, Son of Man, Messiah) are inexact and easily misunderstood. The rest of Mark's Gospel will seek to correctly define what it means that Jesus is the Son of God and Messiah.

Also, Mark will use the rest of the Gospel to develop what these titles for Jesus mean for the Christian community. If Jesus is the Messiah, how should Christians follow him? These few verses, which make it quite clear who Jesus is, are an essential introduction to the rest of the Gospel, which has much work to do yet to lead the readers to a correct understanding of who Jesus is and a correct appreciation of the kind of life that they are called to.

Section 2:
Mark 1:14—3:35

Introduction

In narrative criticism (an important new methodology in biblical studies) the reader pays close attention to the way the author tells the story. Scholars recognize that the importance of the Gospel of Mark is not so much in its historical factuality as in its rhetorical theology. Mark is not trying to tell the reader that Jesus did this deed first and then said this word next, and so on. Neither is Mark trying to say that Jesus spoke exactly these words, and the audience responded exactly this way. Rather, Mark is trying to give the reader an experience of the meaning of what Jesus did and said and how people reacted to him.

Most of all, Mark is trying to give his reader an understanding of how God is at work in the life of Jesus and what that means for Christians and the world. It is in the literary experience of reading Mark's stories that readers are challenged to make the right kind of decisions about Jesus and about the way to live the Christian life. Because of this, readers must pay attention to which stories Mark places together, not because they give us accurate historical information about the sequence of Jesus' actions, but because they give us insight into how to interpret what Mark has to say about Jesus.

In this regard, Mark begins the ministry of Jesus by noting that John had been arrested. On its own, this is not a very important fact for Mark's readers. It does, however, link Jesus' ministry to the ministry of John described in Mark 1:2–8; but, even more important, it allows Mark to foreshadow the passion of Jesus. Mark uses the arrest of John to introduce the ministry of Jesus in order to indicate that Jesus' ministry will arouse the same kind of opposition as John's. Similarly, it is not so important to know that Jesus' first miracle historically was the cure of a demoniac. Rather, it is more important to ask what the placement of this story as the first miracle in Mark's Gospel tells us about Jesus.

The cure of the demoniac makes the connection between Jesus' teaching and his power over demons. In the story of the demoniac, we see the introduction of the issue of Jesus' authority. It is a worthwhile exercise to look up each time Mark uses the word "authority" and examine how important the word is for Mark. Authority is at the heart of who Jesus is.

The story of the healing of a paralytic raises the question of the relationship between Jesus' authority to forgive sins and his power to heal. It also initiates a series of stories in which Jesus experiences conflict and condemnation because of his, or his disciples', behavior (2:1—3:6).

The story of the call of Levi introduces another major theme in Mark's Gospel. Jesus crosses boundaries by breaking the barriers set up in his society. The Pharisees and scribes are shocked that Jesus so openly and willingly eats with sinners and tax collectors. These people were considered by faithful and law-observant Jews to be sinful and unclean. It would have been inappropriate and even damaging to eat with them. The Pharisees question Jesus' disciples about this.

The last section in chapter 3 has a rhetorically important structure. In 3:21 the narrator tells us that Jesus' relatives set out to seize him because they say he is out of his mind. The narrator continues by telling us that the scribes accuse Jesus of being possessed by Beelzebul (3:22). Jesus then refutes this second claim, saying that he could not be working for Satan since he is destroying the power of Satan (3:23–30). The narrator then describes how the mother and brothers of Jesus arrive asking for him and Jesus responds by saying that his family are those who do the will of God (3:31–35). Notice how this section is arranged in concentric parallelism. The two scenes of Jesus' relationship to his family (they accuse him of being out of his mind, and he responds by disowning them) surround a story of the scribes (they accuse him of being possessed, and he suggests that it is they who oppose the will of God). Mark links the opposition of the religious leaders to the interference of Jesus' own family and makes clear that Jesus' ministry will create a whole new family of disciples.

Questions

4. What does Jesus mean when he tells his disciples that he will make them fishers of men? How does this image work?
5. Jesus' first miracle, after calling his disciples, is to cast out a demon. What does that first miracle say about who Jesus is and the nature of his mission?
6. When Jesus casts out the demon, the people are amazed and ask, "What is this? A new teaching—with authority!" How can the casting out of the demon be understood as a "teaching"?
7. Notice how the people contrast Jesus to the scribes. "They were astonished at his teaching, for he taught them as one having authority, and not as the scribes" (1:22). What is Mark trying to tell the reader by setting up such a contrast? What role does having "authority" play in this context?
8. What is the connection between Jesus' authority to forgive sins and his power to heal? Why is the connection important to Mark?
9. What is the role of the scribes and Pharisees in these stories, and do you see a building theme? What is their problem with Jesus? Why does Mark place together a string of five stories that center on this conflict so early in Jesus' ministry?
10. What picture of Jesus does Mark give by having Jesus break barriers and eat with sinners and tax collectors? What is the theological importance of Jesus' response to the Pharisees who question what he does?
11. What is the rhetorical point being made by Mark's construction of a series of stories in concentric parallelism, with the scenes of Jesus' relationship with his family surrounding the scribes' accusation that Jesus is possessed? In what way are these two groups representative of all failures to recognize Jesus?

Conclusions

This section of Mark sets the tone for the Gospel. Jesus is pictured as having the power of God and using it with compassion for those who are suffering and marginalized. He is willing to cross boundaries and break taboos in order to bring the healing and wholeness of God's kingdom to all. In the effectiveness of this ministry, Jesus is contrasted with the scribes. They teach, but their teaching has no powerful effect. Because he acts with the power of God, Jesus incurs the anger and condemnation of the scribes and Pharisees, elders and chief priests, an opposition that will build to the point of their having him executed (like John the Baptist). There is a strong message to the reader to trust in the power of God at work in the ministry of Jesus.

Section 3:
Mark 4:1–34

Introduction

This section introduces a new genre into the story of Jesus—the parable. Scholars have long felt that the parables of Jesus give us a privileged glimpse into the mind and mission of the historical Jesus. However, we must also remember that these parables were translated from Aramaic to Greek and were revised and augmented to serve the teaching functions of the Gospel writers. The parables are not simply the exact words of Jesus as told in exactly the context described in the Gospels.

By definition, a parable is a fictional narrative built on a metaphor that in its exaggeration or twist of reality seeks to tantalize the hearer and encourage reflection on a new understanding of a spiritual reality. Parables do not have a set structure of elements, but in each parable there is some surprising twist in the story that requires the reader to reevaluate previously held beliefs.

Many of the parables, as they come down to us in the Gospels, are clearly allegorical, with elements of the story corresponding to elements of Jesus' religious message. In the first parable and its interpretation, Jesus identifies the seeds with the word, the birds with Satan, and the rocky ground with tribulation or persecution. Yet, even in these allegorical parables, and more so in other parables, the power of the parable is in the lack of a clear and simple correspondence between the metaphor and the spiritual reality. The word is like the seed, but the word is more. Satan is like birds snatching the seed, but Satan's work and power are more. So, in the parable of the mustard seed or the seed growing on its own, the reader must ask what is there about the story and the nature of the seed that is a message for me about the kingdom of God?

What about the seed is like the kingdom, and what about the seed is contrasted with the kingdom?

The parables are not a secret code that, when you learn the code, are simple and clear. Rather, the parables are an ever-challenging experience of being amazed by the kingdom. They call the hearer to enter into a new world, and they demand the listener to constantly reconsider what there is about the kingdom that is like and unlike these simple everyday stories.

This section is comprised of three parables about seeds and an allegorical interpretation of the first seed parable. In the middle of these four seed stories is a parable about a lamp and strong words about the necessity to see and hear. The first parable and its interpretation draw a contrast between the many hindrances for the sprouting seed with the successful harvest of matured grain. There are three fully described impediments that destroy the growing grain. There is also one briefly described context for the successful growing of grain. This grain, however, is hugely successful in three escalating amounts. This contrast between the many possibilities of failure and the almost magical success that is possible would seem to be the focus of these parables.

The parable of the seed growing on its own (4:26–29) focuses both on the inherent fertility of the seed which needs no help from the farmer and the need for the farmer to harvest when the grain is ripe. The parable calls for trusting in the power of God to build the kingdom and for working to "harvest" the fruits of the kingdom. What this balance looks like in the life of the disciple is not explained. The parable challenges readers to seek their own understanding. The parable of the mustard seed (4:30–32) contrasts the original smallness of the seed with its eventual large size. However, the mustard shrub is not even a large tree. It is simply "the greatest of all shrubs." What seems to be its distinguishing feature, however, is that its branches are large enough to provide shade for birds to build their nests. The mustard seed that seems insignificant becomes a large enough shrub to be effective. The kingdom of God is not a great kingdom by material standards, but it is effective in providing sustenance and habitation for those under its canopy.

In this section we get the first hint of the failure of the disciples. Jesus tells the disciples that the secret of the kingdom has been revealed to them, "but for those outside, everything comes in parables; in order that 'they may indeed look, but not perceive, and may indeed listen, but not understand'" (4:11–12). The problem of being blind and deaf to the meaning of the kingdom of God will be a major theme throughout Mark. In this section in both verses 9 and 23, Jesus encourages his hearers, "Let anyone with ears to hear listen!" And we will see, as the story progresses, how the disciples are repeatedly portrayed as having faulty hearing and seeing with regard to the kingdom and the ministry of Jesus. It will be the disciples who are the ones who do not see and hear correctly.

In the recent past, scholars wondered if there was a specific historical context for understanding this theme of the failure of the disciples. Did Mark's community have a historical or social reason to be critical of the historical disciples (the Twelve Apostles) of Jesus? Now scholars believe that this theme in Mark is rhetorical and is meant to challenge readers to learn from the failures of the disciples.

Questions

12. Notice that the first parable is one element of a larger structure. The parable of the seed (4:3–9) and the interpretation of the parable of the seed (4:14–20) frame a discussion between Jesus and his disciples about the purpose of parables (4:10–13). What message about how to hear the parables is Mark trying to give to the reader with this structure? How does Mark use the citation from Isaiah in this discussion to challenge the disciples and the readers/hearers of this Gospel?

13. Why does Jesus tell his disciples to pay attention to what they hear (4:24) and twice command anyone with ears to hear to listen (4:9 and 4:23)? These admonitions are added to his use of the citation from Isaiah, which speaks of looking and listening but not understanding. What is so impor-

21

tant in the parables that Jesus so strongly emphasizes correct hearing?

14. Examine how the image of the farmer and the seed in 4:26–29 works. Consider the contrast between the inactivity of the farmer while the seed sprouts and grows and the immediate need for the farmer's intervention once the harvest is ready. What about the story is like the kingdom of God? What new insights about the kingdom are created by the parable?

15. Examine how the parable of the mustard seed works, and consider the surprising twist in this story. Why is the kingdom likened only to a large shrub? What about the story is like the kingdom of God? What new insights about the kingdom are created by the parable?

16. What do you make of the secret hidden in the parables that is supposedly revealed to the disciples (4:11, 33–34)? Why is it a secret?

17. What is the import of Jesus using all of these seed and growing parables to teach about the kingdom of God?

Conclusions

Notice how the parable discourse is defined as a unit by literary markers. The discourse begins with the narrator noting that "he [Jesus] began to teach them many things in parables" (4:2), and concludes with the narrator telling us that "with many such parables he spoke the word to them" (4:33). Mark focuses the attention of the reader on this first extended teaching given to Jesus' disciples. Jesus teaches his disciples in parables that need explanation, that are difficult to understand, and that are explained to those closest to him. The kingdom of God is not a clear and simple concept. Readers are being told to pay attention to what will be revealed so that they too can understand the message. The readers are being trained to be patient in learning the difficult secret of the kingdom of God as revealed in Jesus. But they are also being told that the kingdom is discovered in everyday life.

Section 4:
Mark 4:35—6:6

Introduction

Mark's description of the journeys that Jesus makes into Gentile territory, especially by crossing the Sea of Galilee, is an important narrative feature in his Gospel. Many commentators see Jesus' frequent crossing of the sea into Gentile territory as symbolic for Mark's community of Jesus' willingness to cross boundaries (ethnic, social, and religious). The first story in this section describes Jesus crossing to the other side, to the territory of the Gerasenes (Gentile territory, east of the Jordan River). The crossing is difficult for the disciples. The storm that terrifies the disciples reflects the terrors they face in leaving their own people and heritage and crossing into Gentile territory to spread the Gospel.

This section, which begins with the disciples in faithless terror over the journey to the other side of the lake, ends with Jesus' hometown in faithless rejection of his healing touch. In the middle are two graphically detailed stories of healings, first of a Gentile demoniac and then of two women. In the first story the demoniac's neighbors, in fear of Jesus' power, ask Jesus to leave, and in the second story the neighbors of the young girl's family ridicule Jesus for believing that the girl's death is not final. All of the stories emphasize the need for trust in God's power in Jesus to bring safety, liberation, healing, and life.

The story of the calming of the storm at sea emphasizes the need for the disciples to trust in Jesus. This story continues the theme of the failure of the disciples introduced in the last section. Jesus' question, "Have you still no faith?" (4:40), points to the goal of the Gospel to train the reader to have faith in God's power manifest in Jesus.

23

The story of the Gerasene demoniac is even more complex than most of Mark's other healing stories (the Gospel of Mark is known for having the most detailed miracle stories). The demoniac is among the tombs and unable to be restrained as he howls and bruises himself. When confronted, the unclean spirit possessing the man claims that his name is "Legion." Any first-century reader would recognize this as the title for a unit of the Roman army. Surely Jesus' healing of this one man has political and economic implications beyond this one person's liberation from oppression, as is reflected by the villagers' fear and request that Jesus leave their village. However, Jesus does not confront the unclean spirit with the same violence that the spirit attacks the man. Jesus' authority over the spirit requires the spirit to name itself and to leave the man. Jesus does not "torment" the spirit as the spirit fears (5:7), but even allows the spirit to enter into the object of its choice. It is an "unclean" spirit, and so it enters into the "unclean" animal, the swine.

Notice that the story of the healing of Jairus's daughter is interrupted by the story of the woman with a hemorrhage. This common Markan technique is called intercalation, i.e., framing one story with the beginning and ending of another story. By placing the stories together (one inside the other), Mark allows the stories to interpret each other. They have more to say about each other than if they were simply one after the other. These two stories are both about women. The woman with the hemorrhage has been ill for twelve years, the age of the young girl. Both women are called "daughter." Both stories emphasize the need for faith. Mark asks the reader to see the connections between the two and find theological meaning in the pairing of the two stories.

The rejection of Jesus at Nazareth serves as a conclusion to this section. The people exclaim over Jesus' "deeds of power" (6:2), three examples of which the reader has just seen. Jesus' reply to their objection that he is only a carpenter and brother to their neighbors gives a justification for Jesus' crossing ethnic, social, and religious boundaries. As a prophet, Jesus is not accepted by his hometown, or even by his own kin and household.

Questions

18. What do the Gentile location of the healing of the Gerasene demoniac, naming the demon "Legion," and sending the demon into a herd of swine tell us about the possible meaning of the story for the original audience? How much does the message and ministry of Jesus deal with political and economic issues?

19. Does the way Jesus treats the demon, Legion, tell us anything about the way Jesus will deal with evil?

20. What is the lesson in the story of the healing of Jairus's daughter made by the fact that Jairus is a synagogue official who comes to Jesus for help?

21. In the story of the woman with the hemorrhage, Jesus does not know who has touched him. (The disciples even chide him for seeking to find the one who has touched him.) How is this an important part of Mark's lesson about the meaning of this miracle?

22. What extra does the framing of the story of the woman with the hemorrhage within the story of the daughter of Jairus add to both stories?

23. When the people of Nazareth compare Jesus' mighty works with his origins and family they take offense at him. What is it that bothers them? Why is Jesus unable to do mighty deeds among them?

Conclusions

The series of stories that show Jesus' power to heal is concluded with a story about his inability to heal because of the lack of faith. The power of Jesus comes up against the one great hindrance to his message—lack of faith. Having faith, or having an intercessor with faith, is a prerequisite for the healings and other mighty deeds. Each of the stories contrasts faith that obtains results in safety, healing, and life with a lack of faith that is lifeless.

The disciples of Jesus furnish two of the examples of lack of faith. They criticize Jesus for his lack of concern for their safety on the boat in the storm, and they criticize him for his concern for the identity of the person who did have faith in his healing touch. Mark uses the disciples, the neighbors from Jesus' hometown, and those gathered for the funeral of Jairus's daughter as examples of the kind of thinking and judging that refuses to trust in a God who can bring healing and wholeness into ordinary lives.

Section 5:
Mark 6:7–33

Introduction

This section of Mark begins with the Twelve being sent by Jesus on a mission and ends with the Twelve returning from their mission. In the middle of the mission of the Twelve is the story of Herod's execution of John the Baptist. The martyrdom of John serves as an interpretive lens for the readers to look at the meaning of the mission of the disciples (and the reader's own mission).

In sending the Twelve out on mission, Jesus gives them authority over unclean spirits. We remember how the Gospel opened with the crowds marveling that Jesus had authority over unclean spirits unlike the scribes (1:22, 27). We can see that the disciples now share in this authority. Jesus also instructs them to take nothing for the journey. This instruction is not simply practical advice. It is the heart of the good news that Jesus preaches. Jesus' disciples are to trust in God's providence and power; they are not to come prepared for every eventuality. The disciples will need no food or money or extra tunics because they will be taken care of by God. Mark is again emphasizing the importance of faith as trust in God. A disciple cannot preach trust in God if their actions do not preach the same message. Mark tells us that the disciples then went and preached repentance, drove out demons, and healed the sick. These three actions summarize the ministry of Jesus so far. They are beginning to follow in the way of Jesus.

The story of the death of John is introduced by the reaction of the people to this expanding mission. Mark notes that Jesus' fame has become widespread. Why is so much power coming from this one man and his followers? The crowds suggest that he is John the Baptist raised from the dead, Elijah returned, or one of the prophets. These suggestions point the reader ahead to the end of Mark's story. Two of the suggestions—John the Baptist and Elijah—are ones who have died or gone to be with God. The possibility of their return points the way for the reader to eventually hear the news that Jesus has been raised from the dead and will return to be with his followers (16:6–7). When Herod concludes that Jesus is John the Baptist raised up, Mark inserts the story of why and how Herod put John to death.

The story of the death of John the Baptist in Mark is graphic and detailed. Both Matthew and Luke shorten this bizarre story considerably. However, in Mark the story is not told for prurient interest in the murderous excesses of the ruling class, but to make a sobering point about the persecution of those who preach repentance, drive out demons, and heal the sick. The reason John is imprisoned is because he told Herod that it was not lawful for Herod to marry his brother's wife. Herod, who fears John and knows him to be righteous and holy, is on the fence about repentance. Herodias, who sought every opportunity to kill John, has turned her back on it completely. This is the message of repentance that John is preaching in 1:4, that Jesus preaches in 1:15, and that now the disciples have been sent out to preach. As they all share the ministry of preaching repentance, they will all share the animosity of those who refuse to repent.

The story of the return of the disciples makes two points. The first point is that they need to take time from their ministry to rest. Jesus encourages them to come away to a deserted place. In several instances in Mark's story of Jesus, Jesus goes away to a deserted place to pray (1:35; 6:46). The word "rest" would be recognized by Mark's readers as comparable to the Sabbath rest shared with God (see Gen 2:2–3). Jesus is encouraging his disciples to share in the prayer that keeps his ministry centered on faith in God. The second point that the story makes is that there is a great desire among the people for what Jesus and his disciples have to offer. Crowds are attracted to the ministry of Jesus.

Questions

24. In Jesus' instructions to the Twelve about how they should go out on mission, what is the message for the reader about trusting in God?
25. How is the story of the execution of John the Baptist related to the mission of the Twelve? How is it both a warning and a consolation?
26. Does the behavior of the family of Herod, Herodias, and Herodias's daughter have any lessons for the new family being created by Jesus? Does the abuse of power and privilege have any lessons for the Christian community?
27. How does the story of the death of John the Baptist foreshadow the story of the death of Jesus?
28. Why does Jesus encourage his disciples to go away to rest after a mission of ministry?

Conclusions

The story of the return of the Twelve sets up the next section. Jesus and the Twelve go off to a deserted place to be alone, but the great crowds follow them. This great need of the people for the leadership authority of Jesus' ministry, which Mark describes as "like sheep without a shepherd" (6:34), reflects back on the failure of King Herod Antipas as shepherd of his people.

Again, we are asked to consider: What is the difference in the way Herod "rules" and the way Jesus exercises the authority he has in the rule (kingdom) of God? What is the difference in the way Herod responds to John the Baptist and the way the disciple responds to Jesus and his apostles?

Section 6:
Mark 6:34—8:21

Introduction

The feedings of the five thousand and the four thousand serve as a frame to enclose this section, with two extra stories related to feeding added at the end. The two stories of the feeding of the multitudes are meant to recall the stories of miraculous feedings in the Old Testament (see Exod 16; Deut 8:3–16; Ps 78:24–25; 1 Kgs 17:7–16; 2 Kgs 4:42–44). The remark that the people are like "sheep without a shepherd" (6:34) recalls the image of the good shepherd in Ezekiel 34: "I myself will be the shepherd of my sheep, and I will make them lie down, says the Lord God....I will feed them with justice" (Ezek 34:15–16).

The section can be outlined as a concentric pattern revolving around the story of Jesus' controversy with the Pharisees over issues of purity (7:1–23). This central story contains Jesus' discussion of clean and unclean foods and what actually makes a person unclean. The first feeding story, of the five thousand, is followed by two stories of miracles that are worked for Jews or that allude to Old Testament stories (the walking on water, which recalls the exodus and Old Testament texts such as Psalm 77:19 and Job 9:8, and the healings at Gennesaret). The second feeding story, of the four thousand, is preceded by two stories of miracles performed for Gentiles (the healing of the Syrophoenician woman's daughter and the healing of a deaf man).

Scholars have suggested that the first feeding is meant as a feeding for Jews (with the numbers five and twelve alluding to Israel of the Old Testament) and the second as a feeding for Gentiles (with the numbers four and seven alluding to the worldwide inclusion of the Gentiles). The central story about clean and unclean foods makes the point that in the new Christian family all foods will be clean (7:19), and so all Christians (both Jews and Gentiles) may share a meal together. Jesus' words to the disciples in 8:19–21 certainly give special significance to the numbers of loaves, recipients, and baskets of leftovers. There is clearly a challenge to the reader to understand some symbolism in these numbers.

Feeding of the Five Thousand (6:34–44)
   Walking on Water (6:45–52)
   Healings at Gennesaret (6:53–56)
   Confrontation with Pharisees over Ritual Purity (7:1–23)
   Healing of Syrophoenician's Daughter (7:24–30)
   Healing of Deaf Man (7:31–37)
Feeding of the Four Thousand (8:1–10)
   Demand for a Sign (8:11–13)
   Yeast of the Pharisees (8:14–21)

The story of the healing of the Syrophoenician woman's daughter (7:24–30) is unique in that Jesus at first refuses to perform the healing. It seems that Jesus objects because the woman is not a Jew and Jesus' ministry is to the house of Israel. However, the Geresene demoniac was also probably not a Jew, living in the Gentile town of Geresa where the major industry was the raising of swine (5:1–20). This story may be designed and placed here to make the point about a mission to the Gentiles.

The story about the yeast of the Pharisees and the yeast of Herod, which ends this section (8:14–21), contains one of the strongest statements by Jesus condemning the disciples for their lack of understanding. In 6:52 at the end of the story of Jesus' walking on the water, the narrator notes that the disciples had not understood the incident of the loaves because their hearts were hardened. The reader is left to wonder what exactly about the incident of the loaves would have helped the disciples understand the walking on the water. Should they have had more faith in Jesus' power? Should they have seen the connection to the Exodus with its miracles of crossing the sea and feeding with manna? Should they have trusted in God's power working in them, since they were challenged in the first feeding to feed the people themselves?

Later in 7:18 Jesus again questions the disciples' understanding. In 8:14 the disciples are on the boat with Jesus, and when he warns them about the yeast of the Pharisees and Herod, they think it is because they have no bread. They are focused on what they lack. Again Jesus condemns them for not understanding, for having hard hearts and for having eyes but failing to see and ears but failing to hear. This is the exact language that Jesus uses in Mark 4 to describe those outside who do not understand the secret of the kingdom. This is one of the strongest statements of failure of disciples in the Gospel and it occurs in the context of what seems to be a call to cross boundaries, transcend purity regulations, and feed both Jews and Gentiles.

Questions

29. What do the Old Testament allusions for the feeding of the five thousand tell us about Jesus and his mission? What are the disciples being called to do in Jesus' words, "you give them something to eat" (6:37)?
30. What do the Old Testament allusions for the story of Jesus walking on water (Ps 65:7; 77:19; 89:9; 107:28–30; Job 9:8) tell us about who Jesus is?
31. What is the connection between the story of the feeding of the five thousand and the story of Jesus walking on water that Mark wants to make for his readers when he notes that the disciples "did not understand about the loaves" (6:52)?
32. What is Jesus' objection to the food laws of the Pharisees in this story? How do you understand the difference between God's commandment and human tradition (7:8)? Why is it important for Mark's community that Jesus declares all foods clean (7:19)?
33. Why does Jesus respond so harshly to the Syrophoenician woman, calling her a dog? Is this story implying that Jesus is challenged by the woman to open up his ministry to Gentiles? Does the woman teach Jesus openness and inclusion?

34. What are "the yeast of the Pharisees and the yeast of Herod" (8:15)? What is the symbolism of the numbers five, twelve, and seven, as well as four and seven, that Jesus points to in his challenge to the disciples' lack of understanding (8:17–20)?

Conclusions

This carefully constructed section revolves around the issue of feeding. The two stories of the multiplication of loaves, the central conflict over clean and unclean foods, the final challenge to the disciples about the yeast of the Pharisees and of Herod, and the symbolism of the numbers involved in the feedings all point to an important message about the role of the disciples in overcoming the boundaries that separate the Christian community, so that all Christians can eat their fill together as one.

Section 7:
Mark 8:22—10:52

Introduction

This section of Mark is also carefully constructed around a theme, this time the three passion predictions. It is a very rich section of the Gospel, arguably the center of Mark's Gospel in terms of its theological importance. The section begins and ends with a story of Jesus curing a blind man. In the first story, the healing proceeds in two stages; in the second story, the healing is immediate. Framed by these two healing stories are the three passion predictions, each of which is part of a similarly sequenced series of stories.

Each passion prediction begins with Jesus informing the disciples that the Son of Man will be handed over, suffer, be killed, and be raised on the third day (8:31; 9:30–32; 10:32–34). Each of these passion predictions is followed by a story of the disciples failing to understand Jesus' mission. Peter objects to Jesus' passion prediction (8:32–33), the disciples are caught arguing over which of them is the greatest in the kingdom (9:33–34), and James and John seek to coerce Jesus into granting them seats at his right and left in his glory (10:35–41).

Following each of these stories of failure is a teaching by Jesus to the disciples on the true nature of discipleship—lowliness, service, and suffering (8:34–38; 9:35–37; 10:42–45). The section can be outlined as follows:

Blind Man of Bethsaida (8:22–26)
Peter's Confession of Jesus as Messiah (8:27–30)
Passion Prediction (8:31)
Failure of Disciples (8:32–33)

Teaching on Discipleship (8:34–38)
Other Stories (9:1–29)
Passion Prediction (9:30–31)
Failure of Disciples (9:32–34)
Teaching on Discipleship (9:35–37)
Other Stories (9:38—10:31)
Passion Prediction (10:32–34)
Failure of Disciples (10:35–41)
Teaching on Discipleship (10:42–45)
Blind Bartimaeus (10:46–52)

The material between the second passion prediction and the third passion prediction seems to have a unifying theme of issues of family. Jesus begins the section by using a child as an example of whom the disciples are to serve (9:36–37). This is followed by a story about an exorcist who does not belong to the family of Jesus' followers (9:38–41). There is a harsh saying about causing one of the little ones (children or new community members) to sin (9:42).

In the center of this section is a saying about marriage and divorce that protects both partners from being abused by divorce (10:2–11). Jesus then becomes indignant at the disciples for rebuking the children who are brought to him (10:13–16). Finally Jesus encourages a rich man to give his money to the poor (10:17–22) and concludes with a full description of the new family that will exist for the disciples who leave their families and possessions (10:23–31). This theme of the "new family" in Mark builds on Jesus' earlier words in 3:35: "Whoever does the will of God is my brother and sister and mother."

Questions

35. What is Mark's purpose in telling the story of Jesus' healing of the blind man of Bethsaida? What could be the symbolism in the healing story about Jesus needing two tries to restore this man's sight completely?

36. How is Peter's confession of Jesus as the Messiah a pivotal moment in the Gospel of Mark? What is Peter confessing?

37. What does Peter object to when he rebukes Jesus after the first passion prediction? Why does Jesus call him "Satan"?

38. What does Jesus mean that "those who lose their life for my sake, and the sake of the gospel, will save it" (8:35)?

39. What is the significance of Jesus' appearing transfigured with Moses and Elijah? Why does the voice from heaven remind the readers that Jesus is God's Beloved Son, repeating the words from the baptism scene?

40. Who is the Elijah figure (Old Testament allusion and person contemporary with Jesus) about whom Jesus says, "they did to him whatever they pleased" (9:13)? What is it that they did to him?

41. How does the story about the boy possessed by a demon (9:14–29) remind the reader of the suffering, death, and resurrection of Jesus? What is the role of faith and prayer in the miracles of Jesus?

42. How does Jesus' teaching while holding a child in 9:35–36 provide a contrast to the attitude of the disciples described in 9:34?

43. What is the importance of Jesus' words about the unknown exorcist in 9:39–40 for an understanding of the inclusive nature of the community of disciples of Jesus?

44. Jesus' words imply that the law of Moses with regard to divorce is not the original will of God. What is the importance of such a teaching on the way we read and interpret the word of God in Scripture? According to Jesus what is the reason given for rejecting the option of divorce?

45. How should we interpret Jesus' words that only those who accept the kingdom like a child will enter it, in the context of this section of Mark's Gospel?

46. Jesus' teaching about riches is one of the most challenging of his teachings. How are we to understand his words that "it is easier for a camel to pass through the eye of a needle than for someone who is rich to enter into the kingdom of God" (10:25)? Consider this statement in the context of Jesus' words that all things are possible for God.

47. Having now seen the repetition of the three passion predictions and their accompanying elements of the failure of disciples and the teaching on discipleship, what is the rhetorical purpose of this repetitive structure?

48. The final story in this section is the healing of blind Bartimaeus. How does this story, paired with the opening story of the healing of the blind man of Bethsaida, form an interpretive frame around the passion predictions? If each of the stories about blind men refers to a stage of discipleship, in what way have the disciples (and the readers) been challenged by the section on the passion predictions to develop from seeing only partially in 8:24 to seeing clearly and following on the way to Jerusalem in 10:52?

Conclusions

This section is the midpoint of Mark's Gospel. The Gospel here moves from a focus on the healing and teaching ministry of Jesus for the people in general, to the more specific training of Jesus' closest disciples. It is this training of the disciples to take up their cross and follow him that serves as a prelude to Jesus' entry into Jerusalem and the beginning of Jesus' passion. It is in this section that we find the strongest and clearest statement of the demands on all disciples to follow Jesus in his way of lowliness, service, and giving his life.

Section 8:
Mark 11:1—12:44

Introduction

This section, which begins Jesus' time in Jerusalem, contains the final stories of controversy between Jesus and the religious leaders (Pharisees, scribes, Sadducees, chief priests, and elders). At first glance, it seems like Mark has simply put together a collection of unrelated stories that feature Jesus in controversy with the leaders over various topics of disagreement. However, upon closer inspection, there are two interrelated themes that are the focus of these controversies: kingship and Temple.

In the first story in this section, Jesus enters Jerusalem on a donkey accompanied by the waving of branches and the singing of Psalm 118. There can be no doubt that the people are greeting Jesus as the Messiah, the returning Davidic king. Jesus himself has instructed his disciples to obtain the donkey in fulfillment of Zechariah 9:9, but it will become clear that their honoring him with cloaks and branches misses the point of why he has come to Jerusalem. At the other end of this section we find the story of Jesus challenging the scribes with a question about the Messiah. Jesus challenges the notion that the Messiah is the son of David, because David himself in Psalm 110 calls the Messiah "lord." With these stories Mark is challenging his readers to see that Jesus is not the kind of Messiah that they expected.

Continuing with this theme of Jesus as the Messiah, there are two stories that focus on Jesus' authority. In 11:27–28 the chief priests, scribes, and elders ask by what authority Jesus is "doing these things." The things that Jesus has just done are: enter Jerusalem as a humble king and cleanse the temple of its animal sellers and money changers. Jesus refuses to answer this question because of the leaders' unwillingness to make a judgment about the origin of John's baptism (heavenly or human). Their indecision shows them to have forfeited their role as religious leaders. This story recalls for the reader the very first public action of Jesus in 1:22, when Jesus taught (by casting out a demon) "as one having authority, and not as the scribes." Jesus is portrayed as having the authority of one commissioned and inspired by God and doing only the work of God. The religious leaders are portrayed as ones protecting their positions, swayed by popular opinion, and motivated by fear.

The second story about Jesus' authority is also telling. The Pharisees (religious leaders) and the Herodians (secular leaders) try to entrap Jesus by asking if the people should pay taxes to the emperor. Jesus' clever but ambiguous reply, "Give to the emperor the things that are the emperor's, and to God the things that are God's" (12:17), reveals much about Jesus' true claim to authority. The scene implies that Jesus' role as Messiah and the authority that God has given him are not essentially political or directed at overthrowing the Roman Empire. Rather, Jesus' authority is directed to the things of God, and is much more of a threat to the religious leaders of Jerusalem than to the emperor of Rome.

The story of the cleansing of the Temple in Mark 11:15–19 is essential for interpreting this whole section. The story is another example of the technique of framing in Mark. The story is preceded by the story of Jesus cursing an unfruitful fig tree and followed by the disciples noting that this fig tree has withered away to its roots. The narrator's remark that "it was not the season for figs" (11:13) makes clear to the reader that Jesus is not cursing the fig tree because he is hungry for figs, but as a symbol of something more important. The story of the cleansing of the Temple provides the clue to interpretation. The fig tree represents the administration of the Temple (the religious leaders of Jerusalem) who have not produced the fruit of true worship of God.

At issue is the business of the Temple. Persons from all over Judea, Galilee, and even the far-flung outposts of the Roman Empire would come to Jerusalem to worship God. To do this they would need to purchase an animal to be sacrificed. The selling of animals fit for sacrifice was a major source of income for the Temple. Also, to pay the half-shekel Temple tax, worshiping Jews would need to exchange their unclean Roman coin (with an idolatrous image on it) for clean Tyrian coin. This exchange also netted the Temple a profit. The administration of Temple sacrifices and Temple taxes had become commercialized. Jesus is not simply clearing out some extreme abuses of the administration of the Temple; he is cutting to the heart of the Temple system. If no one is allowed "to carry anything through the temple" (11:16), the business of the Temple sacrifices and taxes is completely shut down.

As an alternative to this sacrificial activity in the Temple Jesus calls for the Temple to be a house of prayer for all nations (quoting Isa 56:7). In Mark 12:33, a scribe makes a strong allusion to Hosea 6:6 noting that love of God and love of neighbor are "much more important than all whole burnt offerings and sacrifices." The narrator notes that these are wise words and has Jesus commend the scribe as "not far from the kingdom of God" (12:34). The theme of the false reliance on sacrifices, and the worthlessness of sacrifices as compared to love, obedience, and right living is quite common in the Hebrew Scriptures, especially among the prophets (1 Sam 15:22; Ps 40:6–8; Isa 1:11; Amos 5:21–25; Mic 6:6–8). So Jesus' words cannot be construed as anti-Jewish. He is very much in line with a long tradition in Judaism. Since both the sacrificial system and the Temple tax system were exclusively for Jews, Jesus, in keeping with Isaiah 56, calls for the Temple to function for all peoples/nations. Again we see Jesus tearing down the boundaries between Jews and Gentiles and opening up the renewed Israel to all nations.

The story of the widow's contribution to the Temple treasury (12:41–44), while often used as a teaching on generous giving to a religious institution, almost certainly has the opposite meaning. The story is preceded by Jesus' condemnation of the hypocrisy of the scribes who "devour widow's houses" (12:40). The story is certainly not a condemnation of the widow; her generosity is commended. However, in the context of the immediately preceding story and of the whole section, this story offers a strong condemnation of the Temple system that would devour all that the widow, in her poverty, had to live on. The story about which is the first commandment (12:28–34) reminds readers that love of God cannot be separated from love of neighbor (12:33). A system that claims to foster love of God at the expense of destroying the lives of the poor is making a false claim.

The parable of the tenants sits nearly dead center in this section. Many have interpreted this story as a condemnation of Judaism and a statement of Judaism's replacement by Christianity. This is a serious misinterpretation. In the Old Testament it is common for the people of Israel to be pictured as a vine planted by God (Isa 5:1–7; Jer 2:21; Ps 80:8–13). It is also common for the secular and religious leaders of Israel to be condemned for their poor leadership (Ezek 34:1–16; Zech 11:8; Hos 5:1–7; Amos 6:1). Jesus' parable is not directed against Jews; it is directed against the religious leadership in Jerusalem that has failed to provide "the produce of the vineyard" (12:2; see also 11:13–14). This section opened with the crowds chanting Psalm 118 in false expectation of Jesus as the Messiah of Israel who would deliver them from outside oppressors. At the end of this parable Jesus himself quotes Psalm 118 about the stone rejected becoming the cornerstone. In the context of the parable, it is clear that Jesus' role as Messiah is to replace the leadership of Israel and become the one who will produce the fruit of God's kingdom. However, Jesus' role as Messiah is as the rejected one and, as in the parable, the one killed and thrown out. This is not the end of Judaism, but its renewal.

Together these stories offer the reader a chance to reflect more deeply on the exact nature of Jesus' authority and role as Messiah. They call into question false expectations of a Davidic Messiah and false understandings of the purpose of the temple. This section does not present an argument for supercessionism (replacing Judaism with Christianity). Rather, it presents an argument for the renewal of the true heart of Judaism in love of God and love of neighbor.

Questions

49. What is the effect on the reader, in this context of the approaching passion, of Jesus making a prediction about finding the colt and having it come true?

50. Matthew, in his version of this scene, explicitly quotes Zechariah 9:9. Mark probably intends an allusion to the Zechariah text (especially 9:8–10) along with the explicit quotation of Psalm 118. What picture of Jesus as the Messiah is implied by the contrast between the actions and words of the crowd and the prophecy of Zechariah about how the king is to come? What picture of Jesus as the Messiah is offered by the similarities between Zechariah 9:8–10 and Jesus' actions in the temple?

51. Why does Mark place the story of the cleansing of the Temple in the middle of his description of Jesus cursing the fig tree and the disciples finding it withered the next day? How do these three stories help to interpret each other?

52. What do Jesus' teachings on faith, prayer, and forgiveness (11:22–25) have to do with the preceding stories and with each other?

53. What kind of positive message for followers of Jesus is there in the parable of the tenants? What is a possible meaning of the stone rejected by the builders?

54. Is there a general theme about the true nature of God and the correct interpretation of scripture that is found in the collection of controversy stories in chapter 12 (paying taxes to the emperor [12:13–17], the question about resurrection [12:18–27], the greatest commandment [12:28–34], and the question about David's son [12:35–37])?

55. How does the story of the poor widow's contribution fit into its immediate and larger context? What kind of actions and attitudes are being commended and condemned in this story?

Conclusions

This section makes clear and irrevocable the irreconcilable differences between Jesus and the religious leaders. Jesus has laid down the gauntlet and declared the religious leadership bankrupt. With their view of religion, they have no choice but to get rid of him.

He has also presented a clear picture of the kind of leadership that he offers. He is a lowly king, a rejected stone, and a faithful interpreter of God's word. It is ironic that the leadership's attempt to get rid of him will actually install him in his role of leadership. The stone that is rejected becomes the cornerstone.

Section 9:
Mark 13:1–37

Introduction

This section of Mark is often called "the Little Apocalypse" because it describes the events of the end-time and coming of the Son of Man. The image of the Temple ties this section to the previous one. In the previous section, Jesus enters into the Temple as the humble king, proceeds to put an end to the Temple system of sacrifices, and offers an alternative worship of prayer and forgiveness in a community open to all. This section about the end-time distress opens with Jesus' prediction that the Temple will be thrown down (13:2) and defiled (13:14). However, chapter 13 also provides a pause in the building momentum toward Jesus' death.

In chapters 11 and 12, we have seen Jesus enter Jerusalem and engage the leaders in arguments over the Temple and the true nature of the Messiah. This conflict is leading inevitably to Jesus' arrest. However, in chapter 13 the forward movement in Jesus' passion stops, and Jesus offers his disciples, and the reader, advice and warnings about what his coming passion and death will mean for them. The section focuses on Jesus' words for Mark's community, which is in the midst of terrible conflict and uncertainty. Scholars have suggested that Nero's persecution of the Christians in Rome may be the immediate background for the strong sense of persecution in this chapter. The challenge for disciples of all times is to be prepared for this tribulation, and trust in God.

This section begins with the disciples asking Jesus when this destruction of the Temple will happen (13:4) and ends with Jesus' words that only the Father knows the day and the hour (13:32). Jesus, in speaking about the coming catastrophe, warns the disciples not to be alarmed by reports of wars (13:7), not to be worried beforehand about what to say when they are put on trial (13:11), and not to believe the claims of false messiahs (13:21). The disciples are also challenged to beware (13:9, 33), be alert (13:23, 33), keep awake (13:35, 37), and know when the Son of Man is near (13:29).

The chapter describes three negative events. The first is the wars between nations and kingdoms (13:3–8). The second is the persecution of disciples both within and without the community (13:9–13). Disciples will be put on trial in councils, in synagogues, and before governors and kings. They will also be betrayed by fellow Christians (this is probably the meaning of "brother will betray brother to death") and by members of their own family. The third negative event is the appearance of the "desolating sacrilege" (a reference to Dan 9:27; 11:31; 12:11), which requires those in Judea to flee to the mountains (13:14–23). In the context of Jesus' prediction for his disciples, this desolating sacrilege could refer to the Romans entering into the temple, planting their standards, and proclaiming the rule of the Roman emperor at the end of the Jewish War. This is a time of great suffering for all those in Judea.

The chapter then gives three pictures of the coming of the Son of Man. The first is taken from the prophets Isaiah, Ezekiel, Joel, and Daniel. The coming of the Son of Man will be an event that affects the entire cosmos and will involve the Son of Man taking charge of the cosmos "from the ends of the earth to the ends of heaven" (13:27). The second picture is a simple metaphor that compares recognizing the coming of the Son of Man to recognizing the coming of summer (13:28–31). The third picture is a slightly more involved parable of a master who goes on a journey and leaves his slaves in charge of his house (13:34–36). The slaves do not know when he will return and so must be prepared at all times. In both the metaphor and parable the message to the disciples is to keep awake. This is balanced by the earlier admonitions to beware and not to be misled.

An important point made by this chapter is that the coming of the Son of Man will require two things of the disciple. First, the disciple must be prepared to suffer persecution, trial, and catastrophe. Being a disciple who is waiting for the Son of Man does not exempt the Christian from the troubles of the world, persecution by the authorities, or even betrayal by family and friends. Disciples bear the same burden as Christ. Second, the disciple must wait with expectancy and intelligence, always being prepared but not being misled into drawing false conclusions about the coming of the Son of Man. Most of all, disciples are reminded that they cannot know when the time of the end will come. Any prediction of the end is certainly false. Even the Son of Man cannot predict it.

Questions

56. When the disciples ask Jesus when the Temple will be thrown down and what signs there will be of the end, Jesus first warns them not to let anyone deceive them. Why is Jesus concerned that they will be deceived? What is the deception?

57. Why does Mark wait until this point in the narrative to introduce this description of the future suffering of the disciples? How does it help prepare us for Jesus' suffering? How might this description of the suffering of disciples relate to the historical situation of Mark's community?

58. What should the modern reader understand by the prediction of a great tribulation that will be a greater catastrophe for pregnant women and nursing mothers?

59. How does Mark's use of Old Testament allusions (Isa 13:10; Ezek 32:7; Joel 2:10) help the reader understand the meaning of the coming of the Son of Man?

60. How does Jesus' statement that even the Son does not know the day or the hour of the end-time challenge the reader's attitude toward the end-time?

Conclusions

The themes that run through this section are about being awake, being alert, and persevering. Mark's community would have been consoled by Jesus' knowledge of the terrible suffering they were to endure on account of his name, and they would be encouraged to face these hardships with trust in God's Spirit. They would also learn the lesson that the greatest danger in these troubled times is to try to figure out the when and why and how of the end time. Keeping awake and alert means paying close attention to God's plan and not to their own.

Section 10:
Mark 14:1–42

Introduction

A structural feature of this section is the alternation between stories of the forces that bring about or allow the final destructive events in Jesus' life (those seeking his death, betraying, denying, or abandoning him) and the divinely inspired forces that give salvific meaning and effect to these same destructive events. The first story is about the chief priests' conspiracy to arrest Jesus and is followed by a woman anointing Jesus as Messiah before his burial and instead of a burial anointing. The third story describes Judas's involvement in the plan to arrest Jesus and is followed by the other disciples' involvement in Jesus' plan to celebrate the Passover with them.

At the Passover meal Jesus speaks clearly about one of the Twelve who will betray him and then offers the meal as a gift of his very life for their salvation. It is in this section that we see the clear statement of Mark's narrative intention. Jesus notes that "the Son of Man goes as it is written of him, but woe to that one by whom the Son of Man is betrayed" (14:21). Mark wants his readers to know that both the reality and force of evil and the reality and force of good are involved in his death. People must take responsibility for the role that they play.

On the one hand, it is true that Scripture has prophesied that the Son of Man will suffer and die, and God wills that Jesus accept his death. God plans to use Jesus' death to bring about life and salvation for Jesus and all those who belong to him. On the other hand, it is equally true that the religious and political leaders work to arrest and kill Jesus, Judas betrays Jesus, and the other disciples deny and abandon Jesus. Just because God's will uses the death of Jesus for salvation does not absolve the enemies of Jesus of their evil or the friends of Jesus of their failure.

The words of Jesus in Mark make it clear that God does not force the enemies of Jesus to kill him. There is nothing inevitable and required about Judas' betrayal of Jesus. But on the other hand, just because the terrible forces of evil and failure bring about the death of Jesus, that death is still able to be transformed into life by the life-giving power of God at work in all those who seek the good.

Within this structure there are several stories that should be given special attention. Prominent among the stories of the salvific meaning of Jesus' death is the anointing of Jesus by an unnamed woman at the house of Simon the leper. In John's version, the woman is identified as Mary, the sister of Martha and Lazarus, but in Mark and Matthew she is anonymous. However, Jesus' praise of her good work could hardly be greater. Of her good work it is said that "wherever the good news is proclaimed in the whole world, what she has done will be told in remembrance of her" (14:9). Not only does she recognize Jesus as the Messiah, she anticipates and accepts Jesus' impending death; and she suffers persecution for her bold action, which is identified as part of the Gospel message. This marks her as a model disciple. Peter rebuked Jesus for speaking of his impending execution. This woman anticipates Jesus' death and burial with acceptance, love, and compassion.

A theme that sounds strongly in this section is prophecy and fulfillment. In his passion predictions, Jesus has prophesied his coming death and his resurrection. In this section his death looms ever nearer, but his resurrection promise also becomes clearer. The woman anoints Jesus' body for burial because his body will be raised before the women can come to the tomb to anoint him. Jesus foretells how the room for the Passover meal will be acquired, and it comes to fulfillment "as he had told them" (14:16). He prophesies his betrayer in 14:18, and in 14:43 it comes to fulfillment. He prophesies that the Twelve will desert him (14:27) and that Peter will deny him three times (14:30), and in 14:50 all the disciples desert him and flee and in 14:66–72 Peter denies Jesus three times.

To further emphasize the point of fulfillment, Mark has Peter remember the prophetic words of Jesus. This theme of fulfillment is meant to build in the reader a trust in those prophetic words. When Jesus says in 14:28, "But after I am raised up, I will go before you to Galilee" and when the angel reminds the women of this promise "that he is going ahead of you to Galilee; there you will see him, just as he told you" (16:7), readers can trust that these words too have come to fulfillment for the disciples and will come to fulfillment for themselves as well.

The scene of Jesus' prayer in the garden of Gethsemane emphasizes again the theme of the failure of the disciples. Jesus' own faithfulness to the will of God, in spite of being "deeply grieved, even to death" (14:34), is three times contrasted with the disciples' inability to keep awake and pray with Jesus because they repeatedly fall asleep. Three times Jesus predicted his passion, and three times the disciples failed to understand it (chapters 8—10). Three times Jesus prays to do the will of God by accepting his own death, and three times the disciples fall asleep. And, in the next section, Peter will three times deny Jesus, while Jesus is testifying to the will of the Father in front of those who will condemn him to death (14:53–72). Mark wants his readers to see the importance of accepting Jesus' death as the will of God.

Questions

61. Note the irony in the words of the chief priests and scribes as they plan to arrest and execute Jesus: "Not during the festival" (14:2). How does Mark use their words to make a point about the difference between the plans of Jesus' enemies and the plans of God? Why is it essential that Jesus be executed during the festival? What about the meaning of Passover gives meaning to the death of Jesus?

62. What role does the woman who anoints Jesus in Bethany play in Mark's presentation of the meaning of Jesus' impending death? Why will her action (anticipating anointing Jesus' body for burial) be told in memory of her wherever the Gospel is proclaimed (14:8–9)?

63. How does the story of the preparation for the Passover, with its theme of the fulfillment of Jesus' prediction, enhance the message that God's will is being worked out in Jesus' passion?

64. How do the will of God reflected in Scripture and the evil designs of Jesus' enemies work together in Jesus' passion? Why is Judas cursed with a terrible woe even though his actions fulfill the will of God for Jesus?

65. What is the saving value of Jesus' death as stated in the blessings of the bread and of the cup at the Last Supper (14:22–25)?

66. In Gethsemane is the first time Jesus asks his disciples to pray with him. What is the effect on the reader of this request at this point in the story?

67. What does the reader learn by listening to Jesus' agonized prayer? Who is God for Jesus? How does God work? What does Jesus want to happen?

68. What is the effect on the reader of the failure of the disciples at this point? What is it that keeps them from keeping awake with Jesus?

Conclusions

This section cannot really be separated from the next section, as together they form Jesus' passion. However, this section's unique function is to challenge the reader to engage seriously the theological meaning of Jesus' passion and death. In this section of the Gospel, the reader is asked to grapple with the deepest issue of God's power and God's will: the issue of theodicy. How is God's will accomplished with, and in spite of, evil in the world?

Section 11:
Mark 14:43—15:47

Introduction

This section of the Gospel focuses the attention of the reader on the accusations made against Jesus and the treatment that his opponents give him. The reader is asked to recognize the irony in the accusations and in the treatment. They accuse Jesus of threatening to destroy the temple, which is untrue. Yet, in fact, his death and resurrection will make the temple service unnecessary.

They accuse Jesus of claiming to be the king of the Jews, but their view of what this means is distorted. In fact, Jesus is the king of the whole world, but not in the usual way that the world recognizes a king. They mock Jesus for saving others but being unable to save himself. They challenge him to come down off the cross. The truth is that Jesus' power is not for himself but for doing God's will. He saves others because that is the will of God, and he dies on the cross because that is the will of God. Mark's presentation of the false beliefs of Jesus' enemies is meant to clarify for the reader the truth about how God is at work in Jesus' passion.

In the first scene of Jesus' arrest, the contrast is between Jesus' nonviolent acceptance of his fate (made even more pronounced after his prayerful struggle with that fate in the previous scene) and the militaristic preoccupation of Jesus' enemies. First, we note that Judas, identified as the betrayer, counsels the crowd coming to arrest Jesus to "lead him away under guard." Jesus then questions the crowd, "Have you come out with swords and clubs to arrest me as though I were a bandit?" Mark makes much of this ironic contrast, but concludes this scene with Jesus' words that Scripture must be fulfilled. There is no explicit scriptural ref-

52

erence here, but rather the allusion to the suffering of the righteous one in the Old Testament.

The trial of Jesus before the Sanhedrin is paired with the story of Peter denying Jesus three times. Notice how Mark, after setting up the scene of Jesus' trial, notes that Peter is in the courtyard. This is an indication to the reader to think of these two scenes as simultaneous and compare them. The contrast makes the denial of Peter all the more painful. Much has been made of whether this trial before the Sanhedrin, which seems to happen at night, is legal or even historically accurate. Mark's intention is not primarily to give accurate historical information for its own sake. Mark's primary concern in recounting the last days of Jesus is to make a profound point about what kind of Son of God Jesus is.

The next series of four scenes are marked off by a notation of the time of the day: morning, nine o'clock, noon, and evening. In the morning Jesus is brought to Pilate. Mark notes that it is the time of the festival (15:6), reminding the reader of how the chief priests and scribes were concerned not to arrest Jesus during the festival (14:2). This scene also has Pilate realize that Jesus has done no evil, but is only being handed over out of jealousy. We are reminded of the very beginning of the story that sets up the contrast between the authority and power of Jesus and the lack of authority and power of the religious leaders. This story is a contest for the leadership of God's people, and it seems that the chief priests, scribes, and Pharisees have won.

At nine o'clock Jesus is crucified. This scene presents three cases of people reacting to Jesus. Those who are passing by deride him and shake their heads. This reminds us of Psalm 22: "All who see me mock at me; they make mouths at me, they shake their heads." The chief priests and scribes also mock Jesus because "he saved others; he cannot save himself." They challenge him to "come down off the cross now, so that we may see and believe" (15:32). The irony is that it is not his coming down off the cross but rather his death on the cross that proves Jesus to be the Messiah and king of Israel. Those crucified with Jesus also taunt him. (Notice that unlike the Gospel of Luke, there is no "good thief" in Mark's Gospel.)

At noon the scene changes its focus to Jesus himself. Jesus cries out in a loud voice and quotes the opening verse of Psalm 22.

Earlier in 15:24, the note that the guards divide Jesus' clothes by casting lots is also an allusion to Psalm 22:18. Psalm 22 is the perfect presentation of the suffering righteous one who trusts in God. The reader should not dismiss Jesus' painful cry of abandonment as merely the recitation of a psalm. Neither should the reader misunderstand this as a cry of despair. Jesus, in praying/living this psalm, truly experiences the abandonment and pain of the psalmist, as well as his trust and hope in spite of all obstacles.

When Jesus cries again and breathes his last, the Temple curtain is torn in two from top to bottom. The curtain that is torn could be the one separating the court of the Jews from the court of the Gentiles and could signify the opening up of the Temple to all. The curtain could also be the one separating the Holy of Holies from the rest of the Temple. Then the tearing of the curtain might represent the full access to God that is now available in Jesus.

When the centurion sees the way Jesus breathes his last, he says, "Truly this man was God's Son." This is the full recognition of what Mark has been teaching his readers. In seeing Jesus die in this way, mocked, abandoned by all, and crying out to God, the centurion (a Gentile) recognizes that this is what it truly means to be the Son of God. Whether historically accurate or not, Mark uses this Gentile outsider to make the true confession of who Jesus is, a confession that can only come at this moment, when the disciple recognizes Jesus as the humble, suffering servant, obedient to God in all things.

The final scene takes place in the evening and focuses on the good deed of an insider (but an outsider to the disciples of Jesus). Joseph of Arimathea is "a respected member of the council" (15:43). Just as the centurion who crucified Jesus was the first to proclaim his true nature, so this member of the Sanhedrin, which voted for his execution, "went boldly to Pilate and asked for the body of Jesus" (15:43). In Mark there are a series of outsiders (not part of Jesus' circle of disciples) who, against opposition and dishonor, act boldly to do a good deed for Jesus.

Questions

69. How is Jesus contrasted both with those who arrest him and with his own disciples?

70. What is the effect of Jesus remaining silent in the face of the many false testimonies against him, but then answering the question of the high priest, who asks if he is the Messiah, Son of the Blessed One? What does Jesus' mixed quotation of Psalm 110:1 and Daniel 7:13 (in 14:62) add to his statement of who he is?

71. What is the effect of Peter's denial of Jesus immediately after Jesus' testimony to himself?

72. What is Mark's purpose for including the story of choosing between Barabbas and Jesus? Does Barabbas's name ("son of the father") add any symbolic meaning to this story?

73. Notice that in Mark's version of the crowning with thorns, the focus of the abuse is not physical but emotional. The soldiers are described as insulting Jesus more than they cause him any physical harm. Note that the other instances of abuse during Jesus' trial and crucifixion (14:65; 15:29–32) also focus on mockery and insults. What role do these insults play for the reader in coming to understand the truth of who Jesus is?

74. What do Jesus' words from the cross tell us about Jesus?

75. What is the importance of the curtain of the temple being "torn in two, from top to bottom" (15:38)?

76. What is the theological importance of the centurion proclaiming that Jesus, whom he has just crucified, is the Son of God and making this proclamation at just this point in the narrative?

77. What is the role of Joseph of Arimathea, and why is it important for the community to remember him?

Conclusions

This section brings to a close the life of Jesus. The disciples are gone, and the focus is now exclusively on Jesus and his enemies. The reader is now asked to focus entirely on the willingness of Jesus to accept the will of God. But the reader is also made to confront the terrible loss and abandonment that Jesus suffers. It seems as if the whole project of Jesus to inaugurate the kingdom of God has come to nothing. Even God appears to have abandoned Jesus. It is only when the reader can experience the full impact of this abandonment that the true mystery of the resurrection can make sense. God's kingdom comes about through lowliness, suffering, and service. "Whoever loses his life for my sake and that of the gospel will save it" (8:35).

Section 12:
Mark 16:1–20

Introduction

The final section of the original Gospel has only one scene. It is one of the most discussed scenes in the Gospel. The problem with this scene is that it ends so abruptly, with the women saying nothing because they are afraid. This final sentence also ends with the preposition *for*. Even for Mark, whose grammar is not always the best, this is a glaring *faux pas*. Did Mark intend to conclude his Gospel in 16:8 with this sentence ending with a preposition? Or has some original ending of Mark been lost?

Scholars agree that verses 9–20 in the canonical Gospel of Mark were not written by the author of the Gospel but were added to the Gospel in the second century. It is likely that this new ending was created out of the endings of Matthew and Luke because Mark was deemed to be incomplete. Many scholars are now convinced that Mark intended to end his Gospel in just this way for rhetorical reasons—to force readers to make a decision about the story they have just read.

The scene is consistent with Jesus' predictions of his resurrection in 8:31, 9:31, and 10:34. In each of these predictions Jesus says that he will rise "after three days" (another way of saying on the third day). Mark notes that it is the first day of the week, pointing to the beginning of a new creation. Mark also notes that the women who come to the tomb do so in order to anoint him. We noted earlier that the woman of Bethany who anoints him "has anointed my (Jesus') body beforehand for its burial" (14:8). The intention of the women is meant to remind the reader of this earlier scene and the reason for the prior anointing—Jesus' body will not be in the tomb for the postburial anointing.

57

Mark next describes the women encountering "a young man, dressed in a white robe" (16:5). Mark does not describe this person as an angel; in fact, the word Mark uses is the same word that he uses to describe the young man who flees naked from the garden at Jesus' arrest (14:51). Some scholars have suggested that the reader is meant to see the connection. The first young man represents the failure of the disciples who leave everything behind to distance themselves from Jesus and his passion. The second young man represents the restored disciples who will come to believe that "Jesus of Nazareth, who was crucified. He has been raised; he is not here" (16:6). The young man is in the white robe of the newly baptized.

The further message of the young man is to commission the women to go and tell the disciples and Peter that Jesus is going to Galilee to meet them. This recalls the promise of Jesus in 14:28 to go before them to Galilee after he is raised. It is in 14:29 that Peter boasts that even if all the other disciples desert Jesus, he certainly will not. Thus, the young man specifically singles out Peter for this message. So why do the women flee in terror and amazement and say nothing? We will never know for certain, but the ending is certainly a powerful and challenging one.

Like the women, the careful reader can only react to this message with terror and amazement. This is not a feel-good story. This is not what was expected of the Messiah or of God's kingdom. The challenge to a life of following Jesus is a frightening one. Jesus promises his disciples that they will be tested and tried. But there is amazement too that God has brought life out of death and has formed such a great kingdom out of something so small and insignificant. The reader is left with a question, seemingly about the disciples, but more so about him- or herself. Will the disciples go to Galilee to meet Jesus? It is very possible that Galilee represents not the place where the Son of Man will return in victory, but the place where the disciples must begin to live out their version of Jesus' journey in imitation of the Gospel. Galilee is a beginning, not an ending.

In the addition to Mark's Gospel, called the "longer ending" (16:9–20), the text includes several of the postresurrection scenes from the Gospels of Matthew and Luke. However, the text also emphasizes the theme of the failure of discipleship more than do Matthew or Luke. Verse 11 describes how the disciples did not believe the news of Mary Magdalene and is similar to a remark in Luke 24:11. However, Mark 16:14, which has Jesus upbraid the disciples for their lack of faith and for their stubbornness, has no real counterpart in either of the other Gospels. In Luke 24:38, Jesus questions the disciples about "why do doubts arise in your hearts?" And in Matthew 28:17 the narrator notes that when the disciples saw the risen Jesus, "they worshiped him; but some doubted." This expansion of the failure-of-disciples theme in the addition to the Gospel of Mark fits well with the rhetorical strategy of the original Gospel.

Questions

78. How do the women's plans to anoint Jesus and their concern over who will roll away the stone for them challenge the reader to a deeper appreciation of the plan and power of God revealed in the resurrection of Jesus?
79. What role does the young man clothed in white play in the story? What do his words reveal to the reader about Mark's understanding of the meaning of the resurrection?
80. Why are the disciples told to return to Galilee to see the risen Jesus?
81. Why do the women flee in fear and say nothing to anyone?
82. What might the theological message be that Mark intended by ending the Gospel at verse 8?
83. How does the unbelief of the disciples in 16:11 and Jesus' rebuke for their unbelief and hardness of heart in 16:14 fit in with the theme of the failure of disciples in the rest of the Gospel of Mark?

Conclusions

What we know of the original Gospel of Mark concludes with the words of the young man and the reaction of the women. The angel tells the disciples that Jesus is returning to Galilee just as he told them. This reminds the reader of Jesus' words in 14:28. Just as Jesus predicted his death, so he predicted that he would return to Galilee. Many see this as a challenge to the reader to go back and begin again at the beginning of the Gospel (the ministry in Galilee), reading the Gospel anew from the beginning. The disciple is also called now to follow in the footsteps of Jesus' ministry. Having come to understand the necessity of Jesus' death and his resurrection, the disciple can now also minister in Galilee (the world) just as Jesus did.

The reaction of the women is strange and disturbing, but reminds us that this event—Jesus' death and resurrection—is not a simple event to comprehend. The women's reaction reminds the readers how difficulty their own journey to follow Jesus will be.

As noted in the general introduction, it is universally agreed that verses 9–20, while part of the canonical Gospel of Mark (the text that is accepted by the Church as the inspired word of God), are not original to the Gospel. Here we find an initial appearance of the risen Jesus to Mary Magdalene, as in the Gospels of Matthew and John. We also find a scene of Jesus eating with the disciples at table such as in the Gospels of Luke and John. We also find a story of the ascension of Jesus similar to the ones in the Gospels of Matthew and Luke.

Answers

Section 1: Mark 1:1–13

1. When a reader recognizes a biblical allusion (most often by
noting a cross-reference in one's Bible or seeing a mention
in a commentary), the reader should not just find the word
or sentence that is alluded to but should read the whole context of the allusion. Very often the Gospel writer wants to
remind the reader of an entire section of text. The first part
of the quote that Mark attributes to Isaiah is taken from
Malachi 3:1. The prophet Malachi speaks of the coming
time when God will return to the people Israel and cleanse
Israel and its temple. God promises to send a messenger to
prepare the way. Later in the book, the messenger is identified as Elijah, the great prophet of renewal (Mal 4:5). This
quotation informs the reader that the time of John and Jesus
is the end-time when God is coming to cleanse and renew
God's people. When we see John portrayed in ways that
remind us of Elijah (Mark 1:6), we can conclude that John
the Baptist is the Elijah figure who is preparing the way for
God's coming. When we hear that God's spirit descends on
Jesus, we can conclude that Jesus is the coming of God to
Israel to bring cleansing and renewal. The context of
Malachi inclines us to expect a day of power and judgment.

The second part of the quotation is taken from Isaiah 40.
This chapter begins the section known as Second Isaiah
and predicts the return of the people from exile. Isaiah 40
begins with words of comfort to the suffering people of
Israel. In Isaiah, the voice is crying out that a way should
be prepared (either by the hosts of heaven or by the peoples of the world) in the wilderness for the Lord. The
image that is being described is that of a highway to be
built through the wilderness so that God can lead the
people from Babylon back to Jerusalem by the most direct
route (across the impassable desert). In Mark, the voice
becomes John the Baptist who is calling on the people of

Israel to prepare a way for God's coming (by being receptive to cleansing and renewal). Mark has the one crying out located in the wilderness instead of having the way of the Lord being in the wilderness. This makes the quotation fit John the Baptist, who is baptizing in the wilderness, even more exactly. The Lord's coming is the coming of Jesus. While the first half of the quotation points to the cleansing and renewal of the end-time coming of God, this quotation points to the cleansing and renewal of the end of the exile. John is proclaiming that, with the coming of Jesus, Israel's exile from the presence of its God will come to an end.

2. As noted in the introduction, the words from heaven, "You are my Son, the Beloved, with you I am well pleased," are formed from three different quotations from the Old Testament. In Genesis 22:2, God tells Abraham to take "your only son Isaac, whom you love," and offer him as a sacrifice. In Psalm 2:7, God declares to the Davidic king, "you are my son; today I have begotten you." And finally in Isaiah 42:1, God announces that God's servant is "my chosen one in whom my soul delights." "You are my son" comes from Psalm 2, "beloved" comes from Genesis 22, and "with whom I am pleased" comes from Isaiah 42 (the difference in translation is due to the differences between Hebrew and Greek). This collocation of words and images from the Old Testament tells us much about Mark's understanding of Jesus and his mission.

Mark paints a portrait of Jesus as God's own beloved son whom God is willing to sacrifice, as Abraham was willing to sacrifice Isaac in accord with God's command. Jesus is God's anointed one, the Davidic Messiah who is meant to rule over Israel and protect Israel from her oppressors. Finally Jesus is the suffering servant of God, who possesses God's spirit, who does not cry out or shout, and yet who establishes justice on the earth. In the title for the book, Mark introduced his good news about Jesus with the statement that Jesus is the Messiah and Son of God. With this present quotation, Mark tells the reader what kind of

Messiah Jesus is. Jesus is not the kind of Messiah that most were expecting—a powerful king who will lead the people in battle against their oppressors to regain their freedom and create for them a new nation. Rather, Jesus is a Messiah after the type of the offered-up Isaac and after the type of the suffering servant. Already at Jesus' baptism in the first few verses of Mark's Gospel the reader is alerted to the fact that this Jesus, who is the Messiah, will not fit the mold of popular expectations. Yet this is a Messiah very much in line with the Old Testament.

3. Mark's account of Jesus' ministry begins with the announcement by God that Jesus is his son and is followed immediately by Satan's testing of Jesus. This clash between two forces in the life of Jesus summarizes the course of his mission. Jesus' mission is to do the will of God and to confront the temptation of Satan. There is no call of God without also a countercall (temptation) by Satan. What will become central in the Gospel of Mark is how Jesus is faithful to the call of God and how Jesus reacts to and resists the trial of Satan. This story also presents Jesus as a type of the Hebrews being tested in the desert. In contrast to the Hebrews, who were unfaithful to God, who did not trust in God's care and protection, who longed for the fleshpots of Egypt, and who worshiped a golden calf; Jesus trusts in a God who feeds and protects him and resists the temptations of Satan for idolatry, power, and ease.

Section 2: Mark 1:14—3:35

4. This is an odd image: when a fisherman draws a fish out of the water, it dies. However, a common Old Testament image for destruction and eternal separation from God is going down into the deeps of the ocean, the abyss. The sea was the great power of chaos and destruction in the wisdom literature and even in the stories of Noah and the exodus. When Jesus uses the image of catching fish for

catching human beings, he seems to have in mind that his work, and the work of his disciples, will draw humans out of the clutches of chaos, destruction, and eternal death and into the light and life of the kingdom.

5. Mark has deliberately arranged his story so that Jesus' first act is casting out a demon. The demon confronts Jesus and wants to know if Jesus has come to destroy all demons. The demon also declares that Jesus is the Holy One of God. It is striking that Jesus does not destroy the demon, but merely orders it to leave the man. Jesus' role as the Holy One of God is to deliver humanity from the oppression of the demonic. Jesus is concerned with the wholeness of humanity. This story contains many of the important themes of Mark's Gospel. Jesus surpasses the religious leaders because he brings about real healing and salvation. Jesus must confront the forces of evil and command them with power to leave humans. Jesus does not engage in war against evil, but only demands deliverance for humans.

6. Jesus' message in 1:15 is that the kingdom of God is near. Jesus asks his listeners to repent and believe in the good news. The good news is that God has come in Jesus Christ to deliver humanity from its oppression and slavery. The teaching of Jesus is not some new "to do" list of requirements. It is not even the kind of condemnation and challenge that is found in many of the prophets (Jeremiah, for example). The teaching of Jesus is action. The teaching of Jesus is the claim that the power of God is available to deliver humanity from sin, sickness, oppression, and death. That very power is then made present and effective in the ministry of Jesus. This is the good news!

7. This healing takes place in a synagogue on the Sabbath. This is the place and time for the authoritative teaching about God and the administering of God's love and mercy to God's people by the religious authorities. By drawing attention to the difference between the scribes and Jesus,

Mark is preparing the reader for the major conflict that will develop in the Gospel. The religious authorities object to Jesus because his powerful healings, his success with the crowds, and his clever and powerful words show that they, the religious leaders, have been derelict in their duties of ministering to God's people. The question raised by the Gospel is, where is the power of God for salvation manifest among God's people? The answer is in the words and deeds of Jesus.

8. The religious leaders do not have "authority." This author- ity that Jesus has is the effective power, the Spirit-filled power, to bring about the coming of God's kingdom. Jesus is the one who has God's Spirit, and therefore God's author- ity, and in his actions can bring about the kingdom of God in healing and liberation. Authority in Mark does not mean being authorized by the Jerusalem elite, or being trained as a rabbi by the scholarly Pharisees. In Mark, authority has to do with action. Jesus can be recognized as authorized by God because he has the power, in the Spirit, to bring about God's kingdom. For Mark it is very practical. Does your ministry increase the power of sin and suffering or does it bring liberation, health, and God's kingdom? Jesus does the latter and does it so much more than anyone else. All other religious authorities are seen as derelict in their duty com- pared to him. And so Jesus is recognized to have the authority of God. Mark's message is that the power of God is present and available in Jesus and his followers.

9. The story of the cure of the demoniac introduced this sec- tion, which now concludes with a string of five stories that each involves a conflict with the religious authorities. Jesus forgives sins, he eat with sinners, his disciples do not fast, his disciples break the Sabbath by picking grain, and he himself breaks the Sabbath by healing. When one pays close attention to the way Mark is telling his story of Jesus, it becomes clear that the Messiah he is portraying is a Messiah in conflict with the religious authorities. But in

each case of conflict, Mark portrays Jesus as having the correct view. Jesus is more concerned about mercy than about the law. He is concerned to bring God's rule to those in need of it—sinners. He knows the connection between the power of sin and the suffering of humankind and so goes to the source by forgiving sins with the Spirit-filled power of God.

10. In the story of the call of Levi, the Pharisees object to Jesus' eating with tax collectors and sinners. Jesus' reply is that it is the sick that need the physician. He claims that he has come not to call the righteous but sinners. Again we hear the message that was introduced in the first quotation in Mark 1:2. God's reign, which Jesus proclaims, involves healing and restoring a lost, sinful, and suffering Israel. Jesus' ministry is not to lead those who have it all figured out and who are living a godly life. Jesus' ministry is about restoration and healing (a new return from exile). He goes to those who need to be restored and healed. The great scandal is that the very leaders whose job should be to bring healing and restoration to Israel are the very ones who object to Jesus' ministry. God's will is for healing and restoration, and so in hindering Jesus, they hinder God's will.

11. The story begins with the rejection of Jesus by his family who think he is crazy. The story ends with Jesus' rejection of his blood family. He instead forms a new family made up of those who do the will of the Father. In the middle of these two stories is the accusation by the scribes that Jesus is possessed by the ruler of demons, Beelzebul. The scribes' accusation is that Jesus' power over demons comes from evil and not from God. Jesus makes clear the absurdity of this claim. The ruler of evil would not give power to destroy evil. Good comes from God. If Jesus has the power to destroy the oppressive force of evil, then he must have the power of God. Jesus also makes it clear that those who accuse the one filled with the Spirit of God of doing evil are rejecting the work of the Spirit. To accuse the Spirit of

God of being on the side of Satan is an everlasting sin. If you are so filled with fear and hatred and jealousy, trying to maintain your own position in society, that you cannot even see when God's Spirit is at work to bring about good, then you will never be able to see and experience the coming reign of God. This section indicates that the world is being divided in two by Jesus. Those whose preconceived notions about the way things should be (family, religion) keep them blinded to God at work in a new way will never be able to enter the kingdom of God. Those whose preconceived notions of family, honor, propriety, and tradition keep them from recognizing God's anointed one in their family will never be able to be part of the new family created by God's chosen one. This is not a condemnation of Jesus' actual blood relatives as much as it is a challenge to those who seek to be disciples and members of Jesus' new family in any day and age.

Section 3: Mark 4:1–34

12. Sandwiched between the parable and its interpretation is a discussion between Jesus and his disciples. The Twelve question Jesus about the meaning of the first parable, and his answer is very telling. He first says that the secret of the kingdom is given to them, but to those outside everything is in parables. The stance of a disciple is supposed to be one of understanding a secret as opposed to those outside who are confused by the parables. It seems that what identifies a disciple is clear understanding of something that is not clear, something that is a secret, and something that to others appears as a parable needing interpretation. Jesus then quotes Isaiah 6 about those who look and listen but do not perceive and understand. This indicates that the judgment of God is on those who fail to understand what Jesus' message is all about. Finally, Jesus then asks the disciples if they did not understand. The way the question is asked indicates that Jesus expects the answer that they did not understand. He

then asks how they will understand any of the parables. Here is where the theme of the failure of the disciples begins. This question about the disciples' understanding will run throughout the narrative. If they cannot understand the parable of the seed, then how will they understand all the rest of what Jesus says and does? This raises the even greater question of how will they understand the most difficult parable of all, the passion, death, and resurrection of Jesus? The reader is being challenged to pay very close attention to the secret that is being revealed in the Gospel. The reader is being told that this is not a simple story that anyone can comprehend. This story contains a secret that will seem like a parable to those who do not understand it. Only when Mark has made this clear to the reader does he then go on to tell the interpretation of the parable of the seed. Now the reader is prepared to take the interpretation seriously and see its deeper meaning.

13. The chapter on the parables is Jesus' first teaching directed mainly to the disciples, and also to the Christian community reading the Gospel. We have seen Jesus' power over demons and his power to forgive and heal. We have also seen the antipathy that Jesus engenders. This section on the parables challenges us not to draw obvious and easy conclusions from Jesus' power or from the opposition he engenders. We are warned that there is much more to the secret of Jesus' ministry than meets the eye. We are informed that being blind and deaf to God's word was a problem throughout all the history of Israel (as seen in the citation from Isa 6). It is no different now. Seeing and hearing God's word requires much work and attentiveness. Being a disciple requires careful attention to the mechanics of how God's kingdom comes about. Mark's saying about the measure (4:24–25) should not be interpreted as equivalent to Matthew's use of the same saying. In Matthew's Gospel this saying tells the disciples that what they do to others will be done to them (Matt 7:2). But in Mark this saying tells the disciples that the way they go about listen-

ing to God's word and the amount of careful attention they give to God's will, will determine how well the kingdom will grow and bear fruit in and through them. The parables are central to the mission of the disciples because the parables are the statement of how God's kingdom works.

14. The parable of the seed growing by itself features a farmer who scatters the seed and then sleeps and rests. Only when the grain is ripe does the man return to reap the harvest. Sandwiched between, and contrasted to, the planting and harvesting of the farmer is a description of the seed, which sprouts and grows of its own accord. The parable even notes that the farmer does not know how this happens. The growth of the seed is described in stages: the stalk, the head, the full grain in the head.

    The sharp contrast between the farmer who plants and harvests and the seed that grows is a surprise to the reader. It is not actually true that a farmer does nothing after the planting. But the surprising truth to the reader is that the growth of a plant is a miracle contained in the seed. The miraculous vitality and potency of the seed that, when planted, develops into a full-grown plant is compared to the vitality and potency of the kingdom of God. The reader is reminded that the disciple must be willing to "plant" the kingdom in their life (accept it), and will then "harvest" the fruits of the kingdom. But the growth of the kingdom and the producing of the fruits of the kingdom come from the power of God. The disciple does not make the kingdom grow—God does. The disciple only accepts the seed of the kingdom (the Word) into his or her life.

15. There are several points in the parable of the mustard seed that reveal the secret of the kingdom of God. First, the parable emphasizes that the mustard seed "is the smallest of all the seeds on earth," but once it grows it becomes "the greatest of all shrubs." As with much in the parables of Jesus, this is an exaggeration. What matters for the teaching power of the parable is the contrast between

smallest and greatest. Something in the nature of God's kingdom is very small at the beginning, seemingly insignificant, and at its fullness it is large and of great consequence. Second, this parable is based on a parable in Daniel 4, which itself is dependent on a parable in Ezekiel 17. In these parables there is a great tree, which represents a powerful nation and king (in Ezekiel this is Judah, in Daniel it is Babylonia). The great tree, as a symbol of kingship and power, is then cut down to size in both of these parables. In contrast, Jesus' parable tells not of a great tree, but a large plant. This is significant.

The kingdom of God, which Jesus proclaims, inaugurates, and embodies, is not a great tree to rival the kingdoms of the earth. It is only a shrub, but it is a shrub that provides all the sustenance, protection, and support that is supposedly the purpose of a worldly kingdom. In Daniel 4, the great tree of the Babylonian kingdom is supposed to offer shade to animals and a place to nest for birds. But once the judgment of God is made the tree is to be cut down so that the animals will need to flee its shade and the birds its branches. The powerful kingdoms of the earth, portrayed as great and mighty trees, are cut down to size and cannot serve to bring shade and rest to those who need it. In contrast, the kingdom of God has no pretensions to being a great and mighty tree like the kingdoms of the earth. It is only a large shrub, but it does what it needs to do. It serves as a place for the birds to dwell in its shade. The kingdom of God is large in its benefits to those it serves but small and lowly in its worldly claims of power and honor.

16. Jesus tells the disciples that the secret of the kingdom of God has been given to them. The reader expects to find out what the secret is and when it was given. What the reader comes to recognize is that the secret of the kingdom is the Gospel story. While Mark does emphasize the hidden nature of the kingdom, he also emphasizes that knowledge about the kingdom comes from being patiently taught the meaning of the kingdom. Understanding the kingdom does not come

from secret revelation given to the enlightened elect. It comes from Jesus' patient training of very ordinary and very obtuse (at times) disciples in the course of very ordinary lives of service. The secret of the kingdom in Mark is not Gnostic wisdom available only to the enlightened. The secret of the kingdom is available to all who are willing to be trained in this Gospel story by the character of Jesus. The secret is an understanding and a following of the life of Jesus. The life of Jesus in the Gospel is the great parable that all disciples need to come to understand.

17. The parable of the seed is about surprising growth and fruitfulness in spite of all the losses to some of the seed. The parable of the seed growing by itself is about the miraculous vitality and potency of the kingdom that comes from the power of God. The parable of the mustard seed is about the lowliness and humility that characterizes the kingdom and yet its amazing success in serving those who need it. The kingdom of God is a hidden power of life-giving vitality. The parables teach about the humility, lowliness, and nonabusive power that characterize the kingdom. The kingdom will be great, but not like the kingdoms of the world. It will not come by violence and abusive power; it will not be characterized by worldly power, glory, and riches. Rather, fruitfulness, compassion, and meeting the needs of its people will be its hallmarks. The growth of the kingdom depends on the dynamic power of God. The role of the disciple is only to allow the seed of God's kingdom to grow in their lives.

Section 4: Mark 4:35—6:6

18. Gerasa is a town or district on the east side of the Sea of Galilee. It is Gentile territory. In this story, Mark is using geography for theological purposes. Jesus crosses back and forth between the Jewish side of the Sea of Galilee (west) and the Gentile side of the sea (east). Mark narrates the story

in this way to emphasize Jesus' willingness to cross ethnic, religious, and gender boundaries to bring the kingdom of God to all. Mark 5:1 begins by saying that Jesus and his disciples "came to the other side of the sea, to the country of the Gerasenes." They are now in Gentile territory, and this healing will have a message about the Gentiles.

In this story, Jesus confronts a demon that greatly abuses the man he possesses. The man cries out and bruises himself with stones. When confronted, the demon admits that his name is Legion. Any first-century reader would have immediately made the connection to the Roman legions, which were stationed throughout Palestine. It is interesting that Legion asks to be sent into the swine, and Jesus allows it. Pigs were considered unclean animals (ritually unsuitable for food and sacrifice). The sarcastic humor of this story about a demon called Legion entering the unclean herd of swine and running headlong over a cliff and drowning in the sea should not be overlooked.

There is nothing positive in the portrayal of Legion. It seeks to command Jesus to leave it alone, but also portrays itself as the victim that Jesus is tormenting. Mark describes in detail the abuse that the man suffers from Legion. Every audience member in first-century Palestine or Rome would have known of the brutal power of the Roman army legions. They would all know of people who had suffered beatings, shackles, and chains at the hands of the Roman army. For this story to use the name of Legion for a brutal pack of demons certainly makes a clear political statement about the role of the Roman army in the life of the people of Palestine. But the story also seems to imply that Legion need not be massacred or tormented but only told to leave, with their unclean food, the land that is not theirs. It is possible to underestimate the political bite of this story, but it is also possible to twist the point to fit whatever political revolution the reader favors. This story is a sharp political criticism without being a call to violent revolution.

19. The contrast between the way the villagers treat the man

with the demon and the way Jesus treats the man is significant. The villagers (seemingly out of concern for the man
but also out of concern for their own welfare) bind the
man in shackles and chains (5:4). They try to subdue him.
Jesus, instead of trying to control the man, goes to the
heart of the problem and commands the unclean spirit,
which is tormenting the man, to leave. The villagers
shackle the man, while Jesus liberates him. The difference
between the tactics of the unclean spirits and the tactics of
Jesus is also telling. Legion tries to use an oath to keep
Jesus from tormenting them. But there is no indication
that Jesus has any intention of tormenting these spirits. He
asks their name, and, when they beg to be sent into the
swine, he allows it. Jesus does not confront even the
unclean spirits with violence or vindictiveness. Jesus simply
demands that the spirits, which do not belong in the man,
leave the man and go where they belong. They end up
drowning in the sea; their natural home is the abyss. An
important part of how Mark understands Jesus' mission is
that Jesus does not engage in warfare against the demons.
He does not attack them or torment them. He does, however, demand that they free those whom they have bound
in suffering and oppression. The way of Jesus is not to
engage in warfare against evil using the tactics of violence
and might. The way of Jesus is to call on the power of God
to restore people and spirits to their rightful places.

20. The fact that Jairus is a synagogue official can lead the
    reader to draw two conclusions. First, not all of the reli-
    gious leaders are opposed to Jesus. Jesus is open to a per-
    son of faith no matter who they are. Second, the story does
    contrast the power that is available in the traditional reli-
    gious establishment and the power that is available in and
    through Jesus. In the very first healing story (1:21–28),
    the narrator notes that Jesus taught with authority and not
    like the scribes, who seemingly did not teach with author-
    ity. Their teaching did not have effect; it was not accompa-
    nied by mighty deeds and power over demons. This should

not be misconstrued as trying to show that Judaism is bankrupt and has nothing to offer. Instead, Mark is trying to show that the power of the God of Israel is available for Jews and Gentiles alike. God's healing power is not the purview of the religious leaders only, but is available to any and all who trust in God.

21. In this story, Jesus asks who touched his clothes. Both the event itself (the healing seems to happen even before Jesus finds out who it is who has touched him) and the disciples (they ridicule Jesus for even asking this question in such a large and packed crowd) emphasize the oddity of the question. And yet, the time spent dealing with the question indicates that the answer is important. The woman's faith in Jesus has brought about her healing, but more important than her physical healing is her encounter with the one who welcomes her to the kingdom of God. The story makes it clear that seeking out the lost and marginalized and welcoming them into the family of God's kingdom is central to Jesus' ministry of healing and exorcism.

    The story also challenges all disciples to learn from the failings of Jesus' closest disciples. These disciples consistently seek to take the easy way out instead of making the difficult choices for the kingdom. They can't imagine how they will survive a storm, and they can't see how they could possibly find enough food to feed five thousand. They find it ridiculous to even think about trying to find some specific person who touched Jesus in a large and pressing crowd. From their failures and Jesus' calm assurance the reader learns to trust in the power of God and to go the extra mile to make sure that all are included in the kingdom.

22. Several features connect these two stories. The woman has suffered from her hemorrhage for twelve years, and Jairus's daughter is twelve years old. The narrator describes the girl as Jairus's daughter, and Jesus addresses the woman with the hemorrhage as "daughter." Finally, in both stories

Jesus, by touching or being touched by the person, would have been made ritually unclean.

We should also ask if there is any theological importance, beyond these literary characteristics, in the fact that these two stories are joined into one. In the story of Jairus's daughter, Jesus challenges Jairus to move to greater faith. Jairus grows in his awareness of who Jesus is and the power that is available in Jesus. In the story of the woman with the hemorrhage, Jesus is the one who moves to awareness. The woman decides that touching Jesus will heal her; so she touches Jesus and is immediately healed. Jesus is aware of power going out from him but is not aware of who has touched him. Jesus seeks to become aware of the person with the need, the person for whom the healing power was effective. The woman reveals herself to Jesus in fear, and he consoles her with the assurance that it is her faith that has healed her. She might have been fearful that Jesus would be angry because she has made him unclean. She might also be fearful because she has taken the initiative, has touched Jesus, and has gained his power for healing without his permission or knowledge. His words to her inform both her and the reader that she has not taken from Jesus what is his, but has actually accepted in faith what was intended for her. Jesus' words to Jairus are now seen to be parallel. Jesus encourages Jairus to claim for himself, in faith, the healing that will bring his daughter to life.

23. The story of Jesus' rejection at Nazareth emphasizes two themes that recur frequently in Mark—the question of authority and the need for faith. God has given Jesus the authority to teach and do powerful deeds. Yet to some it would seem that because of his background and training he should not have this authority. Frequently in Mark, the leaders and the people call into question Jesus' right to teach and perform mighty deeds. Jesus' neighbors from his hometown take offense (are scandalized) by Jesus because they do not think that he has the authority to do these things. The point of this story is to emphasize that God

gives this authority to those whom he chooses and who trust in him. The good news and power of God's kingdom is now available to those who trust in God. Jesus' neighbors want to restrict this power to those traditionally authorized to use it. Because they reject Jesus' authority, they do not believe in his power or in the power of God working in him. In Mark's Gospel, faith (trust in God) in some form must be present for the working of mighty deeds (it might be a parent having faith for a child, Jesus helping a person with their faith, friends having faith, or the person themselves having faith).

Section 5: Mark 6:7–33

24. It is worthwhile to compare this story (6:7–13) to the first appointment of the Twelve in 3:13–19, where the Twelve are appointed so that Jesus might send them out "to proclaim the message, and to have authority to drive out demons." Jesus does not, at that point, actually send them out. Following the story of the first appointment Mark presents a controversy with Jesus' family and with the scribes. This is followed by the parable chapter of teaching and then the healings of the Gerasene demoniac, Jairus's daughter, and the woman with the hemorrhage. Jesus gives examples of teaching (parables), casting out demons, and healings before he actually sends the Twelve on their mission. The disciples are called to share in Jesus' ministry, but first they must be trained in what that ministry is and how it manifests itself.

    Mark has constructed this story so that Jesus' authorization is followed by instructions for the ministry, which is followed by the narrator's summary of the work the disciples actually do. The center of the story then is Jesus' instructions on how they are to act while on this mission. One suspects that this way of going on a mission (taking no food, no sack, and no money) is actually part of proclaiming repentance. The disciples are required to go from town to town accepting hospitality. It seems that the point of the instruction is not to mandate a life of poverty cut off from the world, but to encourage a life that trusts in God's providence and encourages and celebrates hospitality. The disciples' ministry of trusting in God creates a faith-filled community. Their acceptance in the house they enter is comparable to the belief that greets Jesus when he casts out demons and cures illnesses. This welcoming openness to God's kingdom is part and parcel of the repentance that they are sent to proclaim.

25. Returning to the context of the initial call of the Twelve (3:13–19), we see that immediately after the call of the Twelve, Jesus is accused of insanity and demon possession by his family and the scribes. Even before being shown examples of the message they are to proclaim and the healings they are to perform, the Twelve are introduced to the opposition that the ministry of Jesus engenders. The stories of the sending of the Twelve (6:7–13) and their return (6:30–33) form a frame around the story of Herod's opinion of Jesus and his execution of John the Baptist. The message is clear. Just as the preaching of John the Baptist engenders hatred and plans to kill him, so will the message of Jesus engender hatred from the ruling elite and lead to his execution. The final link in this chain is that the message to be proclaimed by the disciples of Jesus will also bring them to the same confrontation with the forces that detest the power of God to bring healing, wholeness, and justice. Herod's rule is an example of the kind of power that does whatever it wants (6:22–23), which is condemned by Jesus as lording it over people and making their authority felt (10:42). This is the kind of power that disciples of Jesus will have to face in their ministry. By this use of framing stories, Mark makes it clear from the very beginning of the mission of the Twelve that their ministry will be no more "successful" than the ministries of John and Jesus. They also will be hated and sought for execution.

26. Mark's story of Herod serves as a sad contrast to the message of the Gospel of the kingdom of God. Jesus calls his

disciples to become a new family (3:34–35). He calls them to trust in an Abba, a Father for whom all things are possible (14:36). He challenges a father to believe that "all things can be done for the one who believes" (9:23). Later Jesus assures his disciples that "whatever you ask for in prayer, believe that you have received it, and it will be yours" (11:24). Out of the ten healings and exorcisms that Jesus performs in the Gospel, three of them are for parents who bring their children to him. Once Jesus uses a child as an example for the disciples and another time reprimands his disciples for sending parents and children away. Clearly there is something profoundly important in the relationship of parents and children that relates to the kingdom of God. In this story of the martyrdom of John the Baptist we see a father (Herod) who, after seeing a dance performed by his stepdaughter, tells her to "ask me for whatever you wish, and I will give it" (6:22). We see a mother (Herodias) who harbors a grudge against John the Baptist, seeks to kill him, and finds an opportunity in the dance of her daughter. The daughter goes to her mother and asks, "What should I ask for?" (6:24). Herod is a pathetic imitation of a God for whom all things are possible and who wishes to give all good things to his children. Herodias is a pathetic imitation of the parents who come to Jesus and beg his help in gaining healing and liberation for their children. Herodias uses her child to further her evil intentions. Not only does this story inform the reader that discipleship will certainly involve persecution and opposition, it also gives a shocking counterexample of the kind of family that the disciples are called to form. The children of the kingdom of God rely on God to grant all that is good. They seek the health, the wholeness, and the liberation of others. Their ministry is to accomplish the will of God by serving others, not to serve their own ends by using others.

27. The question that introduces the story of the death of John the Baptist is about who Jesus is. The question is about Jesus' power. Some who suggest that Jesus is John the

Baptist raised from the dead explain that this is the reason that "these powers are at work in him" (6:14). Clearly there must be some explanation for why Jesus is so powerful. Herod himself comes to the conclusion that Jesus must be John whom he had beheaded. These reflections point to the reasons Jesus will be put to death—his powers and his authority are a threat to those in power, just as John the Baptist's authoritative condemnation of the sin of Herod and Herodias brought about his execution.

There is also a subtle contrast between the death of John the Baptist and the death of Jesus. The story of the execution of John ends with the note that "when his disciples heard about it, they came and took his body, and laid it in a tomb" (6:29). This will contrast with the story of the tomb of Jesus, when the women come to the tomb and find it empty. The observant reader will note the difference between the entombment of John and the entombment of Jesus. Herod's misunderstanding of who Jesus is (thinking he is John raised from the dead) ironically points to the truth of who Jesus actually is: the Son of God who will be raised from the dead.

28. In the first chapter, the Gospel of Mark describes how Jesus goes off to a deserted place to be alone to pray (1:35). In 6:31, when Jesus beckons the disciples to come away to a deserted place all by themselves, the language recalls the story of Jesus going off to pray. The Gospel of Mark does not emphasize prayer as much as the Gospel of Luke, but it does note three instances when Jesus goes off to pray (1:35; 6:46; 14:32–42). Later, in chapter 11, Jesus will teach the disciples about praying (11:24–25), encouraging them to trust in the power of God. Finally in the Garden of Gethsemane Jesus, while praying, will challenge the disciples to "keep awake and pray that you may not come into the time of trial" (14:38). Given the context after the story of the death of John the Baptist, the time apart for the disciples can be seen as a time of prayer to learn to trust in God so

that when the times of trial do come the disciples will be able to stay awake and alert.

Section 6: Mark 6:34—8:21

29. The feeding of the five thousand recalls the miraculous feeding of the Hebrews with manna and quail in the desert in Exodus 16 and the miraculous multiplication of flour and oil by Elijah in 1 Kings 17. But this story most closely resembles the story of Elisha multiplying the loaves in 2 Kings 4:42–44, where one hundred men are fed with twenty barley loaves, and there is some left over. When readers hear the resonances of these stories they are able to place Jesus in line with Moses, Elijah, and Elisha as mediator of the loving concern and powerful deeds of God. In the Exodus story, the people grumble against Moses and Aaron and accuse them of leading the people into the desert to die of starvation. They do not trust in the care or power of God. Similarly, in the story of the multiplication of loaves in 2 Kings, Elisha tells his servant to give the loaves to the people to eat, but the servant objects that it is not enough to feed one hundred people. Elisha pronounces the word of the Lord that "they shall eat and have some left" (2 Kgs 4:43). In Mark's story, the disciples are invited to give the people food, but they insist that it would be impossible for them to buy the food necessary to feed such a large group. The message in all of these stories is the need to trust in the loving care and mighty power of God. Just as Moses was leading the people to freedom in the Promised Land, so Jesus is liberating his followers from illnesses, oppression, and unclean spirits. Just as the Hebrews in the desert found it difficult to trust that God would provide for them, so the disciples of Jesus continually find it difficult to trust in the power of God manifest in Jesus. The disciples are being called to not only trust in the ministry of Jesus, but also to trust the power of God to work the same ministry in them.

30. Jesus' walking on water, in this context following a miraculous feeding, recalls the power of God that led the Hebrews through the water to safety (Exod 14:21–22). It also recalls Psalm 77:19 and especially Job 9:8, which describe God walking on the waves of the sea. Certainly Mark intends his audience to see in Jesus a new Moses who is delivering God's people from slavery and oppression; but, even more, Mark seems to be implying that Jesus is like the Lord God who has power over the sea and who walks over its waves. This miracle is one of the clearest manifestations of the divine nature of Jesus and the divine power at work in him. The disciples and Mark's readers are being called to trust in a God of care and power who is able to feed and deliver from the waters of destruction, and to see Jesus as the manifestation of God.

31. There are a number of possible connections between the walking on the water and the feeding of the five thousand that could be intended in the narrator's words that the disciples did not understand the multiplication of the loaves. Certainly two of the most important events during the exodus are the crossing of the Red Sea on dry land and the feeding of the Hebrews with manna in the desert. The disciples' inability to understand the multiplication of the loaves would indicate that they do not trust in the God who delivered the Hebrews from Egyptian slavery, and they do not recognize the power of that God at work in Jesus.

Another possible connection between the stories is found in the statement from Jesus prior to the feeding of the five thousand. Jesus tells the disciples, "You give them something to eat." The disciples ridicule the notion that they are to go shopping and pay 200 days' wages to buy enough food for all these people. Yet, it seems that Jesus is actually encouraging the disciples to take the initiative and trust in the power of God. Their fear and lack of understanding when Jesus walks on the water is not because they do not have a high enough opinion of Jesus, but because they do not have a high enough opinion of the power of God to work in themselves. Scholars point out that Jesus calls to the disciples with the words, "it is I," which remind the reader of the revelation of God's name in Exodus, "I am." In this reading the lack of understanding of the power of Jesus in the feeding is compounded in their failure to recognize Jesus as the "I AM." This points to the disciples' failure to appreciate the person and power of Jesus.

32. When we look at this story, we notice that Jesus does not set out to preach against the Jewish food and purity laws. He only defends his followers from accusations of breaking the tradition of the elders. (The "tradition of the elders" refers to the oral law passed down among the Pharisees that for them has the same force as the Mosaic Law.) Jesus defends his disciples by accusing the Pharisees of hypocrisy because they place more emphasis on human traditions (Jesus would seem to imply that the "tradition of the elders" does not have the force of God's law found in the Torah) than on God's commandments. The example he uses to show their hypocrisy is the commandment to honor one's father and mother. According to the tradition of the elders, the financial support due one's parents could be given as a dedicated offering to God. Jesus interprets this as failing to keep the fourth commandment. How is this an answer to the situation of not washing one's hands? Jesus' principle of interpretation is to measure a practice against the original intention of God's law. The purity rules of Leviticus are all based on the principle that the people of God are called to be holy as God is holy (Lev 11:44). This is the principle that all purity rules must be measured against. The holiness of God is not an external holiness; so the holiness that God's people are called to cannot be merely an external holiness. The rules of Leviticus were intended to create a people committed to the holiness of God. Jesus asserts that washing one's hands is not integral to this intention, but purity of heart is. Washing one's hands does not form a person in the image of the holy God, but cleansing one's heart of evil intentions ("fornication, theft, murder, adultery, avarice,

wickedness, deceit, licentiousness, envy, slander, pride, folly" [Mark 7:21–22]) does. Just as dedicating your property to God does not fulfill the fourth commandment, so washing your hands does not fulfill the command of Leviticus to be holy as God is holy.

The observation by the narrator in Mark 7:19 that Jesus "declared all foods clean" is a statement central to the meaning of this section. The Jewish ritual food laws required that they eat only kosher foods. Jews were not permitted to eat the food of the Gentiles or even to eat with Gentiles. By declaring all foods clean, Jesus effectively abolishes any boundary between Gentile Christians and Jewish Christians. Now all can sit down to the Supper of the Lord together. We know from Galatians 2 and Acts 10 that these very food laws posed a major threat to the integration of the Jewish and Gentile Christian communities. The two multiplications of loaves, one for Jews and one for Gentiles, indicates that the disciples are called to create a community that feeds all its members, Jews and Gentiles.

33. This is one of the most perplexing stories about Jesus. One possibility for understanding Jesus' insult to the woman is to see some false sense of entitlement and even injustice in the woman's actions. Jesus is in an area with many Jewish residents who would have been second-class citizens. This woman is a first-class citizen. The story may imply that the woman's actions could be seen as another form of the elites' abuse of the lower classes by demanding that Jesus do a mighty deed for her. Jesus does not insult her because she is a Gentile but reminds her that God's first concern is for the lowly, oppressed, and marginalized people of God. Her words to Jesus indicate that she understands this principle. She knows that his gift of healing her daughter would be only a scrap that falls from the table, while the table is reserved for poor and oppressed Israel.

Other scholars have suggested that the story is meant to show Jesus' own growth from a Jewish prejudice against Gentiles to a new awareness of the needs of Gentiles. The woman's words help Jesus to see more inclusively. This may be stretching the idea of Jesus growing in his understanding of his ministry, but it does point to the importance of the inclusion of Gentiles that is central to this whole section. Gentiles need to be fed too. This story makes that clear.

34. There are two possible interpretations for the symbolism of the two feedings. Both interpretations agree that Mark has arranged the material and placed these words of Jesus at the end in order to focus the readers' attention on the symbolic point that is being made. The first interpretation focuses on belief. Jesus can feed more people with less bread and more leftovers in the first miracle because of belief. He feeds less people with more bread and less leftovers because of increasing unbelief. This unbelief is the yeast of the Pharisees and the yeast of Herod. This interpretation builds on the comment of the narrator in 6:5 that Jesus did not perform any deeds of power in Nazareth because of their unbelief.

   The second interpretation says that the numbers associated with the first feeding (five and twelve) are numbers associated with Judaism (five books of the Law and twelve tribes of Israel), while the numbers associated with the second feeding (four and seven) are numbers associated with the Gentiles (four corners of the earth and seven signifying the completeness of the whole world). Jesus is teaching the disciples to feed both Jews and Gentiles. Jesus' mission crosses boundaries and is for all peoples. Those who hold this interpretation observe that the two miracles following the feeding of the five thousand are Jewish miracles and the two miracles immediately before the feeding of the four thousand are miracles performed for Gentiles. The story in the center of this section concerns the washing of hands and clean and unclean foods. In that story, Jesus declares all foods clean. This declaration would destroy the barriers forbidding Jewish Christians and Gentile Christians from eating together.

Section 7: Mark 8:22—10:52

35. Those arguing that the numbers in the previous story signify increasing unbelief see the healing of the blind man of Bethsaida as proof that unbelief is the issue. But the story does not refer to the issue of unbelief. In the outline of Mark given in this book, the healing of the blind man of Bethsaida is the beginning of the section of passion predictions and, together with the concluding healing of blind Bartimaeus, forms a frame around that section. Certainly Mark is not trying to show that even Jesus makes mistakes in his healing. And probably Mark is not trying to show that Jesus has trouble with this healing because of the increasing unbelief among those following him. When we read this section as a carefully constructed unit trying to make a point for the reader, we can see that Mark is using the sight of the blind man of Bethsaida to represent the sight of the disciples. Peter, as the spokesman of the disciples, sees that Jesus is the Messiah but can't see clearly what that means and therefore rejects Jesus' prophecies of his passion. Jesus then leads the disciples through three sets of passion predictions with accompanying failures of disciples and teachings on discipleship. Finally the section ends with blind Bartimaeus being healed immediately and following Jesus on the way (to Jerusalem and to his death). This story indicates the full sight that should have been gained from the teaching of the passion predictions.

36. With Peter's confession that Jesus is the Messiah in 8:29, the focus of Jesus' ministry in the Gospel changes from miracle stories directed at the general public and controversy stories directed at the scribes and Pharisees to an extended section of teaching directed at the closest disciples. Peter's confession of Jesus as the Messiah is clearly a great insight into the true nature of Jesus, but Jesus also warns the disciples not to tell anyone about him. This is an instance of the Messianic Secret theme in Mark. We have seen already how Jesus tells the demons not to reveal who

he is and those healed not to tell anyone about him. It is all part of the same theme. Mark is informing the reader that there is something more to the nature of Jesus that is not yet understood. The demons who know Jesus as the Holy One of God, those healed who can testify to his divine power to heal, and even now the disciples who recognize him as God's chosen Messiah, do not fully understand Jesus and what his mission will entail. The secret of Jesus and his mission will become clear to the reader in this next section. Jesus is the suffering Messiah whose mission will lead to his arrest and execution.

37. Peter rebukes Jesus for his public prediction of his passion. It is not yet clear in the story what Peter objects to. The reader must fill in this gap. As we read the rest of this section, we learn much about the thoughts of the disciples. They argue over who is greatest in the kingdom, and when James and John ask Jesus for the privilege of sitting at his right and left in his glory (the positions of most honor and power in Jesus' entourage) the rest of the disciples are indignant (they want the same thing for themselves). It becomes clear that Peter (representing the thinking of all the disciples and even the reader) is rejecting the way of the cross. He thinks of Jesus as the chosen Messiah of God who has been given the power of God to heal, drive out demons, restore life, and bring all the blessings of the kingdom to those who follow him. Peter looks to Jesus to restore the fortunes of Israel by liberating the people from the oppression of the Roman Empire, by restoring correct worship to the temple, and by inaugurating the kingdom of God. He expects a renewed kingdom of David, with Jesus as the anointed king and his disciples in positions of honor and power. It is a very attractive vision. There is not one follower of Jesus who does not at some time or other wish that God in Jesus would just destroy all evil and bring all blessings with a stroke of power.

The great scandal of the cross is that God does destroy the power of evil and bring all blessings but not with a stroke of power but, rather, with the way of the cross, the way of service, lowliness, and suffering. The disciples are not offered positions of honor and power but are offered the same way of the cross that Jesus must travel. By having Jesus call Peter "Satan," Mark lets the reader know that this temptation in all of us to desire the easy way, the way of honor and power, is the most dangerous temptation there is to the kingdom of God that Jesus brings. Jesus does not call the unclean spirits or the religious leaders "Satan." They oppose his mission to bring about the kingdom of God, but they do not pose the same threat to the kingdom that the desire for honor and power in the disciples poses. The profound message in the Gospel of Mark is that the real danger to God's kingdom is found in the hearts of the disciples, not in the threats of Jesus' enemies.

38. Two important principles become clear in this first teaching about discipleship (8:34–38). The first is that when disciples proclaim the good news of God's kingdom, they will find themselves at odds with the power structures and the religious authorities. They will be arrested, tried, and executed for the message they preach. The second principle is that all attempts to mitigate this situation of persecution by changing the message, keeping quiet, trying to work with the authorities (14:43–44), fleeing (14:50–52), lying (14:66–72), or even fighting (14:47) will only backfire. There is no salvation in these attempts to save one's life. Those who, like Jesus, accept their fate and go to their deaths will, like Jesus, be raised to life by God. This is the only salvation there is: the life that God gives.

39. Following immediately after the passion prediction, failure of the disciples, and teaching about discipleship, the transfiguration makes an important point about the connection between Jesus' passion and his glory. Jesus is in the company of Elijah and Moses. Elijah was the great prophet and wonderworker who was taken by God in the fiery chariot to be with God (2 Kgs 2:11) and was expected to return in

the last days to prepare for the coming of God (Mal 4:5–6). Moses led the people from slavery in Egypt and received the Law from the hand of God. It is easy to see Elijah and Moses together representing the prophets and the Law, the totality of God's word to Israel. By appearing with Jesus in glory, Moses and Elijah indicate that Jesus fulfills the prophets and the Law and will, therefore, be rewarded with heavenly life (like Elijah and Moses) because of his role in God's plan of salvation. But the stories of Moses and Elijah are also stories of suffering and persecution. Elijah has to flee for his life from Jezebel (1 Kgs 19:1–4), and Moses flees from pharaoh (Exod 2:15) and is later grumbled against by his own people (Exod 16:2). The stories about Elijah and Moses and their significance in the salvation history of Israel provide the context for our understanding of Jesus.

It is significant that immediately after Jesus' first passion prediction and teaching on discipleship, in the context of the three passion predictions, the voice from heaven (God) reminds the disciples (and the readers) that Jesus is God's Beloved Son and to listen to him. That the voice tells the disciples to listen to Jesus is particularly important in this context. Jesus is teaching about the way of the cross, the way of lowliness, service, and suffering. This is what it means to be the Son of God. This is what the disciples must learn. This is what was revealed in Jesus' baptism when he was immediately driven out into the desert to be tempted by Satan. Jesus was there forty days, reminding us of Elijah being in the desert forty days while being pursued by Jezebel, and Moses being on Mount Sinai forty days while receiving the Law.

40. As noted previously, Malachi 4:5–6 expects Elijah to return at the end of time to prepare the way for the coming of God. Jesus is claiming that now is the time predicted by Malachi. John the Baptist is Elijah returned, and Jesus is the coming of God to bring about the restoration of God's people. But unlike more traditional expectations of end-

time restoration that present a scene of judgment and military might, Jesus speaks of the returning Elijah suffering at the hands of those in power as preparation for the coming of God. And he speaks of the Son of Man (Jesus) also suffering greatly and being treated with contempt. In traditional interpretations of Malachi, the coming of Elijah and the coming of God were manifestations of power that would set all things right. In Jesus' reinterpretation of Malachi, the coming of Elijah in John the Baptist and the coming of God in Jesus are marked by lowliness, service, and suffering. The coming of God at the end time, the coming of God's kingdom, is not a coming with power, but with suffering and service.

41. The story of the boy with the demon is one of the most complex and rich miracle stories in Mark. The suffering of the boy is described three different times in the story before Jesus actually confronts the demon possessing the boy. The father first describes the suffering of the boy, then the narrator describes what the demon does to the boy when they bring the boy to Jesus, and finally in response to a question from Jesus, the father describes the demon's attempts to kill the boy. Given that this story occurs in the context of the three passion predictions, it is tempting to see the threefold description of the suffering of the boy as parallel to the threefold prediction of the suffering of Jesus.

    The story also focuses on the faith that is required for healing. The father asks Jesus to help if he can. Jesus replies with the enigmatic, "If you are able!" Is Jesus mocking the man for even thinking that Jesus might not have the power? Or is Jesus challenging the man to himself have the faith necessary to perform the miracle. In that case, the "you" in "if you are able" would be the father. This is a distinct possibility as the father cries out that he does believe and asks for help in increasing his belief. This interpretation is confirmed by Jesus' statement that all things are possible to the one who believes. Jesus challenges this father and all disciples to trust in a God for whom all things are possible (14:36).

Earlier Jesus challenged his disciples to feed the crowds themselves (6:37) and told the woman with the hemorrhage that it was her faith that saved her (5:34). Jesus is training those who follow him to accept the authority that God has given to the Son of Man and to trust in the power that God has made available to all through Jesus.

The story ends with a discussion between the disciples and Jesus about why the disciples were unable to cast out the demon. Jesus tells them that this kind can only come out through prayer. This teaching is probably not trying to distinguish different kinds of demons and different modes of exorcism. Rather, this teaching is about the use of God's power in general. God's power, made available to all through Jesus, is a power accessed by faith (trust in God) and this faith is only gained by turning to God in prayer. This power is not available for one's own use. Only by turning to God in faith and by accepting the will of God, even as you know that all things are possible for God, does one have power over the demonic. The definition of the demonic is power without obedience to the will of God. The final lesson of this rich and complex miracle story is about the importance of prayer for turning to God in faith.

42. In the second grouping of passion prediction, failure of disciples, and teaching on discipleship (9:30–37), the disciples react to Jesus' passion prediction first with a lack of understanding and then with an argument among themselves over which of them is the greatest. Jesus' teaching centers on lowliness and service. Jesus points to the child not as an object of emulation (later in 10:15 he does encourage accepting the kingdom of God like a child), but as an object of care and attention. The lesson is that the attitude of the disciples in their mission must be similar to the attitude of parents (especially mothers) in their care for children. The model of what it means to be great in the kingdom of God is not the powerful elite of the kingdoms of the day, but the loving family whose attention, energy, and resources are used to bring their children to a healthy

maturity. The disciples must think of themselves as loving parents giving their lives for the welfare of their beloved children. There is no room for self-aggrandizement and competition for power in such a situation.

43. John's report to Jesus about someone who was exorcising in Jesus' name without Jesus' authorization may indicate the disciples' desire of exclusive rights to this power of God. Jesus rejects this thinking. This story presents a profound statement of the democratization of God's power. Jesus asserts that "whoever is not against us is for us" (9:40). The disciples do not control the power of God to bring about God's kingdom. God's power is available to all who call on God in faith. All who do God's will (giving a cup of water to those who belong to Christ) will be rewarded by God. There are no other requirements for doing God's will and accessing God's power than trusting in God and desiring to do the will of God.

44. Jesus' saying on divorce indicates that the word of God in Scripture cannot be read literally and slavishly. The word of God needs interpretation in the context of God's original intention. Jesus indicates that the Law of Moses regarding divorce was promulgated because of the historical and social situation of the people's needs and desires and did not reflect God's will for humans. Jesus does not reject the Law of Moses as the word of God, but he does indicate that it must be interpreted in a larger context. It is historically conditioned, and it must be judged in terms of how well it reflects the will of God. So in 2:23–28, after a discussion of the law regarding working on the Sabbath, Jesus concludes, "The sabbath was made for humankind not humankind for the sabbath" (2:27). In other words, there is a hierarchy of values. The law about the Sabbath does not have value on its own as a law to be obeyed. The law about the Sabbath was instituted to give human beings rest, to honor their work and their value, and to allow them to share in the glory of God. When the Sabbath does

not do these things, but rather makes life worse for humans, then the Sabbath law should not be obeyed. The law of divorce is interpreted even more negatively. Jesus concludes that its institution was a mistake from the beginning, and the original intention of God concerning marriage is to be found in Genesis 2.

45. Given all that Jesus has said about caring for children as the model for the mission of the kingdom, what does it mean in 10:15 that the disciple is to accept the kingdom as a little child? It could of course mean that the disciples should accept the kingdom as they accept the child, but that would be redundant after Jesus has made that same point earlier. It may be that Jesus' image is meant to work in two directions. Jesus has taught the disciples that they should work for the kingdom as if they were caring for their own children. Now he tells them that they should see the attitude of children toward their parents as the kind of attitude that they need to have toward the kingdom of God. They need to trust in God, rely on God, and turn to God for their life and growth. The little child thus becomes the model for how to think about ministry and how to think about one's relationship to God. No wonder family images are so plentiful in this section. The kingdom of God can only be understood as a family whose members trust in a loving Father and who treat each other with the selflessness, care, and concern of a loving parent.

46. The man in this story asks what he must do to inherit eternal life, and Jesus answers that he must keep the commandments. This the man does. The conclusion would be that this man will inherit eternal life. However, he is seeking more. In recognizing this man's desire for more life, Jesus loves him. This story is not about a new commandment of Jesus, which, if not observed, will lead to eternal death. This is about Jesus' offer to the man to share more deeply in God's offer of life, to be an active part of the coming of the kingdom. Because of his riches, the man is

reluctant to give all to join in the spreading of the kingdom of God. Jesus notes how hard it is for those with many things to let go and follow the way of the lowly, suffering servant. The disciples are astounded and seemingly misinterpret this encounter. They wonder who can be saved.

Nothing in the conversation between Jesus and the rich man indicates that he will not be saved. Is entering the kingdom of God the same as inheriting eternal life? Mark uses the story not to condemn the man as unable to inherit eternal life, but to challenge his community to a life that allows for the fullest blossoming of the kingdom. That kind of life is a life that lets go of all possessions—land, house, family, honor, and goods. Even when the disciples make the claim that they have done this, Jesus reminds them that part of the "reward" they will receive is persecution. The central point of this teaching is that it is the power of God that makes all things possible, and human perfection comes through letting go of all we cling to.

47. It is important after examining individual stories in depth to step back and see the larger picture. It can be argued that this section is the central teaching on discipleship in the Gospel of Mark. The repeated predictions of Jesus' passion emphasize the importance of the passion for understanding who Jesus is and what his mission is about. The three examples of the failure of the disciples that follow each of the passion predictions emphasize the all too frequent tendency of Jesus' disciples (of all times) to be concerned with glory, power, and their own place in the community. The three teachings on discipleship all emphasize the importance of lowliness, service, and suffering. It is clear that for Mark the teaching that his community needs to hear is the teaching on lowly service. Jesus is a lowly, suffering, and serving Messiah, and all disciples are called to this same path. This teaching is the most difficult message for Jesus to communicate to his disciples, and probably the most difficult message for modern Christians to accept as well.

48. Having seen the message of the three passion predictions and the accompanying teachings about discipleship, it is easy for the reader to see that the stories of the two blind men represent two stages of discipleship. The disciple who follows Jesus, believes in his God-given power to heal and cast out demons, and seeks to work for the kingdom with the same God-given power, but who misunderstands this mission as one of honor and power and success is like the blind man who only sees partially. After hearing the teaching on Jesus' passion and the true calling to a discipleship of lowliness, service, and suffering, the disciple who is willing to follow Jesus on the way to Jerusalem, the way of the cross, and emulate Jesus' ministry of lowliness and service is like blind Bartimaeus who is healed immediately and follows Jesus on his way.

Section 8: Mark 11:1—12:44

49. In the latter half of Mark there are two notable instances of Jesus giving instructions to the disciples that involve a prediction. In both cases the predictions are fulfilled. In this scene Jesus tells the disciples to go into the village where they will find a colt tethered. He tells them what to say if anyone questions them. They find the colt as he predicted, and to those who question them "they told them what Jesus had said" (11:6). Later in chapter 14 Jesus will give instructions on how to find a place where he and his disciples will celebrate the Passover, and the disciples find "everything as he had told them" (14:16). The purpose of these two predictions, with their immediate fulfillments, is to confirm for the disciples and the readers that Jesus' predictions will be fulfilled.

As we saw in the previous section, Jesus' predictions of his passion and his resurrection have not been easily understood and accepted by the disciples. The lesson in this story is that just as the disciples find the colt as predicted and will find the upper room as predicted, so they will find Jesus risen just as predicted. One of the most important attributes of a disciple for Mark is trust. The disciples have been trained to trust in God's power to heal, to raise from the dead, and to calm storms. In the previous section of the Gospel the disciples were being trained to accept the suffering service of the lowly Messiah. Now they are being trained to trust his word that not only will he suffer and die but that he will be raised by God to new life. As the Gospel of Mark ends, the reader has only the word of Jesus (which the young man at the tomb repeats) to rely on. Jesus predicted his resurrection. The young man confirms that Jesus has been raised (16:6) and reminds the disciples that Jesus "is going ahead of you to Galilee; there you will see him, just as he told you" (16:7). The ending of Mark leaves much to be explained and experienced. There is no risen body to see or touch, no apocalyptic events to signal a great miracle. There is only a statement of a prediction fulfilled. For the careful reader who has learned to trust in Jesus' word (and the power of God), this is enough to set them on the road to Galilee where they will see the risen Jesus.

50. In Zechariah 9:9 the prophet proclaims to Jerusalem, "Lo, your king comes to you; triumphant and victorious is he, humble and riding on a donkey, on a colt, the foal of a donkey." In Zechariah 9:8 God announces that "I will encamp at my house as a guard, so that no one shall march to and fro." This fits with Jesus' action in the Temple in the next scene when "he would not allow anyone to carry anything through the temple" (11:16). In Zechariah 9:10, the prophet says that the new king "shall command peace to the nations." Mark is using the prophecies of Zechariah to create a picture of the kind of Messiah Jesus is. Jesus is the meek and humble Messiah whose mission is to bring peace and offer salvation even to the Gentile nations.

51. This is another example of Mark's tendency to place one story in the middle of another story. The story of the cursing of the fig tree and its subsequent withering is interrupted

by the story of Jesus cleansing the Temple. Scholars have long noted the importance of this structure for interpreting the message of the story. Even taking the cursing and withering of the fig tree by itself, the careful reader will note clues that this story is not to be taken literally. The narrator notes that it was not the season for figs. It is unlikely that Jesus would curse a tree for not having figs when it was not fig season. This leads the reader to understand that there is something more going on with this story, and this deeper meaning is clarified in the story of the cleansing of the Temple. The fig tree represents the leadership and system of the Temple. It does not produce the fruit that it should. Jesus condemns those running the Temple for making it a den of thieves.

In the next chapter Jesus tells the parable of the tenants, which again condemns the present leadership of God's people; and in chapter 13 Jesus predicts the destruction of the Temple. It is fairly clear that Jesus' action of cursing the fig tree symbolizes his condemnation of the Temple and its leadership. The question is why? Jesus' quotation of Isaiah 56 points us to Mark's intention in this story. In Isaiah 56:3, the prophet says, "Do not let the foreigner joined to the Lord say, 'The Lord will surely separate me from his people.'" Isaiah 56 is focused on God's commitment to include fully among God's people all non-Jews who seek the Lord. Jesus' critique of the Temple is not just about monetary exploitation and fiscal abuse. Jesus' concern is that the requirements of purity and Temple sacrifice have become a means of excluding Gentiles from worshiping the Lord.

52. Some have suggested that Mark has included the sayings on prayer and forgiveness at the end of the story of the fig tree because of the catchwords "faith/believe." However, there is an even further connection between Jesus' saying about prayer and forgiveness and the cursing and withering of the fig tree. The story of the cleansing of the Temple (as part of the cursing and withering of the fig tree) condemns the Temple system and implies that it has run its course and

will no longer exist as part of God's kingdom. This raises the question of how do you have your prayers heard and how do you obtain forgiveness when there is no Temple? The Temple was the place where people joined together to petition God and offer sacrifices and oblations. The Temple was the place where the people of Israel could offer sacrifices to bring about forgiveness and the place where the whole nation offered sacrifice on the Day of Atonement.

Jesus' clearing sacrifices from the Temple raises the question of how could God's people stay in right relationship with God without the Temple and its system of prayers and sacrifices? The answer that Jesus gives is that you do not need the Temple to pray. All you need is to trust in God and pray. What you pray for will then be granted to you. Prayer does not need to be mediated by the Temple system. A second question is how can one obtain forgiveness from God if one does not complete the requisite sacrifice in the Temple, and how can the people of God obtain forgiveness without celebrating the Day of Atonement? The answer is that the people of God, in forgiving one another, are forgiven by God. The Temple sacrifices and the offering of the scapegoat on the Day of Atonement are replaced by the community's action of forgiving each other. Not only does Jesus clear the Temple this one time, he teaches his followers how to pray and forgive in such a way that the Temple system is no longer necessary.

53. This is a disturbing story, especially if it is taken too allegorically, making the vineyard owner, God; the servants, the prophets; the son, Jesus; and the tenants, the Jewish leaders. In this interpretation, God sent his son Jesus to the Jews who rejected and killed him, and so God will reject and kill the Jews and give the kingdom to the Gentiles who will produce fruit. This has been the common interpretation of the parable, but this picture of God is not in keeping with the rest of Mark's Gospel.

It is clear, though, that the parable provides a condemnation of the chief priests, scribes, and elders (12:12). They are the keepers of the vineyard (Israel) and they have not fostered it. They reject God's plan. And yet, what they reject as unworthy becomes the cornerstone in God's renewed people. This parable should not be used as proof that Christians, and not Jews, are God's chosen people. Instead, it should offer a challenge to all God's children not to reject too quickly what does not fit with their plans. God works in the unlikeliest places with the unlikeliest of materials.

54. The controversy stories in chapter 12 all point to a God whose concern is for the well-being of God's people. In each of these stories, Jesus' opponents misinterpret Scripture by focusing on a literal interpretation rather than on seeking to understand God's intention for the law. By questioning Jesus about paying taxes to Caesar, the opponents are trying to invoke the first commandment, but Jesus will not be caught in their trap. Even though Caesar may claim to be God, to pay taxes to Caesar is not tantamount to denying the one true God.

In another story, the Sadducees focus on the absurdity of a hypothetical example of a woman having seven husbands in the resurrection, instead of seeing in Scripture that God is a God of life who will bring new life to God's people. Next, one scribe comes near to the kingdom of God by recognizing that love of God cannot be separated from love of neighbor. God's will in the law is human well-being. Finally, Jesus challenges the current obsession with a new Davidic king, a Messiah in the style of David. Using Scripture, Jesus shows that God's chosen Messiah will be greater than David. God's plans far surpass the hopes and expectations of the people. Perhaps a good summary of Jesus' message in this section is found in 12:24: "you know neither the scriptures nor the power of God." The Sadducees' method of interpretation of Scripture and their expectations of God are shallow and confined to the literal and everyday. God's plan for the kingdom, and God's power to bring it about, surpass any of their expectations.

55. The story of the poor widow who gives her whole liveli-
    hood is often interpreted as a positive example of selfless
    giving. Certainly the widow can be commended for her
    generosity, but it is likely that this story is much more than
    an example of generosity. The previous story (12:38–40)
    condemns the scribes because they "devour widows'
    houses." The story of the widow's generosity must also be
    seen as a story of the abusive nature of the Temple system
    that requires even a poor widow to give all she has to live
    on. It is one thing for the Temple system to take the sur-
    plus wealth of the rich, but quite another for it to take the
    livelihood from a poor widow. Given its context, this story
    cannot be read simply as a story of generosity. The story
    challenges the reader to see the conflict that can exist
    between a false "love of God" that becomes abusive to
    neighbor and an authentic love of neighbor.

    In the previous story, the scribes "devour widow's houses"
    and at the same time "for the sake of appearance say long
    prayers" (12:40). Jesus' condemnation of the scribes
    exposes a false love of God that is coupled with an abuse of
    neighbor. In the story about which is the first command-
    ment (12:28–34), the saying about the love of God and the
    love of neighbor is concluded with a subordination of burnt
    offerings and sacrifices (quoting Hos 6:6). The examples of
    violation of the covenant that are cited in Hosea 6 are
    ambush and murder. In other examples of the subordina-
    tion of sacrifice among the prophets, the issues most often
    contrasted to hypocritical worship are justice, goodness,
    and doing right. Jesus' concern that an authentic love of
    God must be coupled with true love of neighbor is a theme
    already found throughout the prophets.

Section 9: Mark 13:1–37

56. First, it is clear that the disciples still do not have the same
    view of the world that Jesus does. They are impressed by the
    great architecture of Herod's Temple (and who wouldn't

be—it was one of the Seven Wonders of the World), but Jesus is not impressed. This building, like all human efforts, will come to an end. The disciples then want to know the signs of the end-time so they can be prepared. Jesus warns them about this attitude. They are again trying to have control over events that are in God's control. The danger is that they will be led astray and duped in their rush to figure out what is happening. Jesus speaks to two dangers. The first is that they might believe that someone other than Jesus is the returning Messiah. And second is that they will be frightened by wars, earthquakes, and famines. Jesus' point seems to be the exact opposite of the message many modern Christians read into these verses. Jesus tells his disciples that there will be wars and earthquakes. Don't be led astray into thinking that the end-time is coming immediately. These things just happen. But most of all don't grab for a quick Messiah, whether that be an ideology, a person, or a military or political policy. False messiahs, false expectations, false solutions are the real danger in the kind of thinking that characterizes the disciples: trying to be the first in line for the end-time.

57. This chapter paints a rather bleak picture of the life of the Christian, and probably gives us a glimpse of the suffering and persecution experienced by Mark's own community. Mark's community in Rome would probably have suffered some of these events during the reign of Nero, when he blamed the Christians for the great fire in Rome. It is not that this description would have scared Mark's community if it had been placed earlier in the Gospel. This was their experience. Rather, only now, at this point in the Gospel, could the community understand what this suffering of theirs meant. Only now could they see their own experience as sharing in the experience of Jesus and as what Jesus predicted for them.

At this point in the Gospel they have been trained to trust in the power of God, so they can trust with confidence Jesus' words that "the one who endures to the end will be saved" (13:13) and that "for the sake of the elect, whom he [God] chose, he has cut short those days [of suffering]" (13:20). Having been prepared by the Gospel to trust the power of God and to know the coming death of Jesus, Mark's community can now see their own suffering in the larger context of God's plan of salvation. They are ready to go with Jesus on the way of the cross and experience Jesus' passion in all its terror and pain.

58. Probably the most important point to take away from this saying is that there will be terrible suffering in the lives of Christians, and that God cares and will see that God's chosen ones are saved. Some have suggested that this saying reveals the reason Jesus chose not to marry. Because he expected the end time to come with catastrophe and pain, he chose to be celibate. For Jesus, the present was the time to witness to the Gospel and not the time to raise a family. For the modern reader, the call to celibacy is not motivated by the imminent end of the world. Some disciples are called to the complete focus on the ministry of the Gospel that celibacy allows, and many are called to raising a family in conformance with the Gospel. It will always be the case that very difficult decisions arise pitting commitments to family against commitments to the Gospel.

59. Mark begins with the quotation from Joel. In Joel 2 the prophet is warning the people of Israel that the coming of God is not what they expect. They were expecting God's coming to bring honor and victory to Israel and defeat and punishment to Israel's enemies. The prophet warns the people that God's coming requires repentance. It will not be a day of joy and victory but a day requiring repentance and prayer. Even in Isaiah and Ezekiel, where the prophecies are directed against the enemies of Israel (Babylon and Pharaoh), the focus of their condemnation is on the sin of pride and abuse of power. The point of Mark's using the quote from Joel is not to describe the physical meteorological phenomenon that will accompany the return of the

Son of Man, but to challenge the reader with the purpose of the Son's return. The Son of Man will return to gather God's people who have been called to repentance. The end-time coming of the Son of Man is not to wage war against Israel's enemies or form a mighty kingdom. The end-time coming of the Son of Man is to gather a chosen people who have trusted in God. The message of this story in Mark is not about punishment of God's enemies, but about the repentance and prayer required of the disciple to be prepared as one of God's chosen.

60. From the beginning of this section, where Jesus warns the disciples about being deceived, to the end, where he explains that no one knows the day or hour of the end, Mark is cautioning his community not to engage in speculation about the end. Jesus describes the trials and suffering that will be the lot of Christians, he promises the care and salvation of God for those who endure, he explains the need for repentance to be a part of God's chosen ones, and he exhorts his disciples to pay attention to the will of God and be alert to what God is doing. But this section in no way gives a play-by-play description of the end of the world. That kind of speculation will only lead the disciple astray. The surprising statement of Jesus that even the Son does not know the day or hour also reminds the reader that the life of the Christian, in imitation of Jesus, is concerned with the here and now. The Christian life is not founded on some future event of God's coming but on the present kingdom of God.

Section 10: Mark 14:1–42

61. The claim of the chief priests that they will not arrest Jesus during the festival is a good example of Mark's use of irony. The chief priests believe that they are the ones in charge during the arrest, trial, and crucifixion of Jesus, but Mark makes it clear that God is the one who is ultimately in

charge. That does not mean that God arranges to have Jesus put to death. God does not put Jesus to death, but it is God's will that Jesus accept this death. It is also God's will that the death of Jesus show forth the true meaning of Jesus' sacrifice. The death of Jesus will happen on the feast of Passover to show that Jesus' obedience to the will of God inaugurates a new Passover.

Passover is the celebration of God's deliverance of the Hebrews from slavery in Egypt. The Passover lamb is sacrificed, and its blood placed on the doorposts of the Hebrews so that the angel of death will pass over the houses of the Hebrews and their firstborn sons will not die. The meal that is shared that night joins the community into a people obedient to God's will and a people ready to respond to God's call. Jesus' words at the Last Supper point to that symbolism. His blood is given so that his followers may live; his meal is shared as food for the journey. Notice how Jesus and the disciples after the meal immediately set out for the Mount of Olives, just as the Hebrews set out for Mount Sinai.

62. The woman at Bethany anoints Jesus for his burial before his death because there will be no opportunity to anoint him after his death. When the women come to anoint him in 16:1, Jesus is already raised. But what is perhaps most significant is that the woman anoints Jesus' head with oil. This points more to a messianic (kingly) anointing than to a burial anointing. The point being made is that in his death Jesus is made (anointed) God's chosen Messiah. The argument about money and the poor only serves to highlight the importance of this action.

Also, this woman is the first in a series of outsiders (non-disciples) who will do a good deed for Jesus at his death. These outsiders will point to the true nature of discipleship—lowliness, service, and suffering. This selfless service to Jesus and to all those who belong to Christ (see 9:41) is the hallmark of the disciple. To train disciples to act as this woman acts is the purpose of the Gospel. This story is central to the

Gospel message because it imitates the selfless service that characterizes the passion and death of Jesus.

63. This is the second story that centers on a prediction of Jesus coming to fulfillment. The first was the story of the procurement of the colt in Mark 11. In the present context, which contrasts the will of God and the will of Jesus' enemies, this story emphasizes the power of God to bring to fulfillment what has been foretold. The finding of the upper room is not simply a clever trick showing that Jesus knows the disciples will meet someone who has an upper room for rent. The point of the story is to train the reader to trust that God is in control of these events. God has foretold that the Messiah will suffer and die. These events will happen, not because of the power of the enemies of Jesus, but because of the will and power of God.

64. Jesus' words at the beginning of the Last Supper identifying the betrayer are central to understanding this section of Mark and to understanding the theology of the whole Gospel. The focus of this story is to emphasize that it has been prophesied and it is God's will that Jesus, the Son of Man, will suffer and die. But it is also true that the one who hands Jesus over to his death is culpable of a great evil. Just because Judas's action is made a part of God's will for Jesus and is used in God's plan to bring about the salvation of God's people does not mean that the act is not evil and that Judas is not responsible for this evil. Jesus' words that "the Son of Man goes as it is written of him, but woe to that one by whom the Son of Man is betrayed" (14:21) make it clear that these two realities must be held in tension. Jesus' suffering and death are the result of culpable evil on the part of people whose actions will be punished; at the same time, Jesus' death has been predicted by Scripture and is part of God's plan of salvation. The truth of either one of these does not make the other untrue. This is the great and complex issue of theodicy. How can God be all powerful and all good and still allow evil?

The Gospel does not give a philosophical answer. However, the force of Mark's entire narrative is to convince the reader that both these realities are true. God is all powerful and all good, and, in God's power and goodness, God even uses the evil of human decisions to bring about salvation and new life. But this does not exonerate those who choose evil actions, which God transforms into new possibilities for good.

65. With his blessing of the bread and cup in Mark, Jesus offers the bread and cup to his disciples as his body and his blood. What Jesus has to offer his disciples is his life, and his life is one of giving himself in service and in suffering. When James and John ask for seats of honor, Jesus offers them his cup and his baptism. Jesus does not offer glory or even an easy solution to life's problems (Mark does not have the saying that is in Matt 11:30: "For my yoke is easy, and my burden is light"). Jesus offers a way of life in obedience to God's will. In Mark the Eucharist is not a sharing in a divine food that magically fixes all one's ills. The Eucharist is a sharing in the life of Jesus, which is doing the divine will in suffering and service.

Jesus continues by saying that his blood is the blood of a new covenant. In the context of this as a Passover meal, these words remind us of the covenant God made with the people in the exodus. In Mark, Jesus gives his life for the sake of all, and he offers this meal with his disciples as a way of offering them his life, which is the reality of a new relationship (covenant) with God. Jesus' life is the relationship of the Son to the Father. In the context of this feast, there is a profound reinterpretation of the Passover story since this Son does die (unlike the Hebrews' firstborn sons), but, by the power of God, death is overcome.

66. Jesus has taught his disciples in chapter 9 that prayer is necessary for casting out demons. He has taught them in chapter 11 that all they ask for in prayer will be given them. Jesus himself has gone off to pray at significant points in his

ministry (1:35; 6:46). Now in this final climactic day of Jesus' life, he asks the disciples to accompany him as he prays and to keep awake and pray with him. Remember how important being alert and awake was in Jesus' teaching about the end time in chapter 13. It is as if the training of the disciples and the mission of Jesus come together at this point.

The message is that prayer is essential when the disciples must grapple with terrible suffering and persecution. It is during this toughest of times that the disciples must most imitate Jesus and turn to the Father in prayer and listen for God's will to be made known. Prayer in Mark is intimately tied to suffering and death. Prayer is about discovering the will of God in the midst of pain, persecution, and catastrophe. Prayer does contain an element of asking to be spared the terrors of these times. (Jesus prays for the cup to pass him by and encourages the disciples to pray that they might not undergo this time of trial.) But an even more important aspect of prayer is coming to accept the will of God as Jesus does: "not what I want but what you want" (14:36).

67. This is perhaps the most powerful scene in Mark's Gospel. Throughout the Gospel we have seen Jesus' anger and frustration at his enemies and his compassion toward those in need. We have also heard Jesus calmly predict his passion and resurrection. But this is the first time we have seen Jesus have emotions about his own personal situation. Jesus' profound emotions about his own impending suffering and death take us by surprise and challenge us to take seriously the call of service and suffering. This story is a stark portrayal of Jesus' interior battle between the two competing aspects of trusting in God. He acknowledges God the Father as his Abba (therefore loving and good) and as having power to do all things. But he also acknowledges that God's will might not be to save him from death. This is the great struggle all believers have. If God is good

and all powerful, why do these terrible things happen? There is no simple answer.

Jesus simply holds both his belief in God's goodness and power and his own willingness to do the will of God in perfect balance. It is clear to the reader that God hears the prayer of Jesus but does not "answer" it at this time. It is the will of God that Jesus must die. It is not the will of God that this cup can pass Jesus by. But for Jesus and for Mark, God's will that his chosen ones suffer and die does not negate God's power or God's goodness. It is only in prayer that these two truths can be held together properly.

68. The fact that the disciples fall asleep when Jesus is engaged in this agonized prayer, grappling with the most profound issue of all human life, forces the reader to remain with Jesus and identify with Jesus. But at the same time, it challenges the reader to consider what in their own lives causes them to "fall asleep" and miss the important signs of God's will. Jesus tells the disciples to "keep awake and pray that you may not come into the time of trial; the spirit indeed is willing, but the flesh is weak" (14:38). Chapter 13 focuses on the importance of keeping awake and alert. The disciples are to pay close attention to the signs of the times.

This story describes how the disciples could not keep their eyes open. It would seem that their sleep is symbolic of their unwillingness to keep alert in the sense of chapter 13. What is it that keeps them from being alert and prepared? Jesus indicates that it is because the flesh is weak. What does this mean? The seed parable of chapter 4 might offer a clue. In that parable, those who do not produce fruit are those who, because of trouble and persecution, fall away, or who have the word choked by the cares of the world, the lure of riches, and the desire for other things (4:16–19). This also helps us to interpret what keeping alert means in chapter 13. It probably does not mean being alert for signs of the end, as much as for signs of God's will in the midst of tribulation and persecution, in the midst of concerns for this world, and in the midst of temptations to selfishness.

Section 11: Mark 14:43—15:47

69. At Jesus' arrest, Judas tells the crowd to "lead him away under guard" (14:44). The crowd of people, sent by the chief priests to arrest Jesus, comes with swords and clubs. Jesus even mocks them saying, "Have you come out with swords and clubs to arrest me as though I were a bandit?" (14:48). One of the bystanders even takes up the sword to defend him. Jesus stands in contrast to all these military weapons and physical violence. He has already submitted to doing God's will. He recognizes that this arrest is so "that the scriptures be fulfilled" (14:49). The way that the story is told emphasizes the contrast and makes the military might and violence of the chief priests absurd and foolish. Military might is not how God works.

70. Something of the same contrasting theme is going on at Jesus' trial. The trial is an effort of the chief priests and the entire Sanhedrin to look for testimony. Many give false testimony, but they don't agree. In contrast to this flurry of intrigue and deceit, Jesus stands calmly and does not respond. Again, the way the story is told mocks the vain attempts of the Sanhedrin to convict Jesus with their lies. Only when asked directly if he is the Son of the Blessed One does Jesus honestly proclaim that he is. All the intrigue and deceit of the Sanhedrin is for nothing when Jesus calmly proclaims who he is. The point is that Jesus will be convicted, not by false testimony and trumped-up charges, but for the truth of who he is: God's chosen Messiah, God's beloved Son.

71. Another contrast is drawn in the story of Peter's denial of Jesus (14:66–72). As Jesus calmly proclaims that he is the Messiah and Son of the Blessed One, an admission that will get him crucified, Peter denies even knowing Jesus (seemingly out of fear of being arrested too). Many scholars believe that during the persecution of Christians in Rome under the reign of Nero, some Christians would betray

other Christians and some would deny that they were Christians. So the stories of Judas and Peter are not written simply as historical remembrances but as examples that offer comfort and insight for the experience of the Christian community in Rome (and disciples of all times). The message would seem to be that even those closest to Jesus fled from persecution and denied their faith, but they were rehabilitated later by the risen Jesus. Those who deny being Christian under persecution can be forgiven. The story of Peter's denial does not serve as a condemnation of Peter but as a lesson in discipleship.

72. There is nothing in this scene that indicates that Barabbas is not a historical figure, but it is interesting that his name means "son of the father." This again sets a contrast with Jesus and focuses attention on Jesus' claim to be Son of God. He is chosen over Jesus, who is the true Son of God the Father. Jesus is hated and rejected precisely because of his claim to this relationship with God. And as Pilate recognizes, the chief priests hand Jesus over out of jealousy (15:10).

73. The insults are much more important for Mark's Christology than physical abuse would be. Mark is not trying to teach his audience that Jesus has saved God's people by suffering more physical abuse than anyone else. Mark is trying to teach his audience that Jesus is the lowly, servant Messiah, who saved God's people by his selfless service and willing acceptance of the will of God. His death is important not as paying some price by suffering, but as accepting the will of God and dying in service to others. To make this point Mark uses the taunting words of the soldiers, the passersby, the chief priests, and the others crucified with Jesus. All mock Jesus for his claim to be someone important: prophet, king of the Jews, Messiah. They want to know why if he saved others he cannot save himself.

Mark does not dodge this hard-hitting and important question. In fact, Jesus is what all the mockers ridicule him for. He is the Messiah, king of the Jews, and a prophet. He did save others; he did foretell the destruction of the temple. And he cannot save himself. God alone saves. Jesus saves others with the power of God and in prayerful obedience to God. He cannot save himself, if it was not God's will. His enemies want him to prove that he is who he claims to be by saving himself, but it is actually in his being fully obedient to the will of God (and thus not saving himself) that he shows himself to be the Son of God, Messiah, and king.

74. Jesus words from the cross (*"Eloi, Eloi, lema sabachthani?"*) are a quotation from Psalm 22. Some scholars believe that the reader should interpret Jesus as praying the entire Psalm 22, and so hear a psalm of trust in God and an expectation of salvation. Other scholars believe that the whole scene points to Jesus praying only these words, which express his anguished cry of feeling abandoned by God. We cannot pretend to know the mind of Jesus at his death, and Mark's account is ambiguous. What is clear is that even in his great anguish and even if feeling completely abandoned, Jesus calls out to God who is his Abba and cries out with the words of Scripture. He turns to a God who has spoken promises to God's people. Mark allows us to see enough of Jesus' heart to know that Jesus is deeply anguished about his fate and the seeming absence of God. We know that Jesus was grieved to death at the prospect of his execution. But Mark also makes it clear that even in this moment when all seems lost, when there is no visible hope, and when God seems to have abandoned Jesus, Jesus turns to God and prays the words of the inspired psalmist. This is not despair; this is being obedient to the will of God.

75. When Jesus dies, the curtain of the Temple is "torn" in two from top to bottom. The same word is used at Jesus' baptism when the heavens are torn open. The curtain that Mark has in mind is either the curtain that separated the public areas from the areas that only Jews were allowed to enter or the curtain that closed off the holy of holies.

Either way, it seems that the tearing of the curtain indicates that Jesus' death opens up the Temple and makes God available to all. This would fit with the story of the cleansing of the Temple, where Jesus, quoting Isaiah 56:7, says, "My house shall be called a house of prayer for all the nations" (Mark 11:17). In Jesus, access to God is no longer restricted but is opened up to all.

76. The text of Mark 15:39 says that when the centurion saw how Jesus breathed his last, he makes his confession that Jesus truly was God's Son. It is important who says this and about what. It is significant that the climactic proclamation of who Jesus is comes not from one of his disciples, but from the man who has crucified him. Mark has been trying to convince his readers that the way of lowliness, service, and suffering is not only the will of God but also the power of God at work. Jesus' humble death, with its cry to God, transforms the centurion from an executioner to an apostle. It is also significant that Jesus is only recognized truly at this point in the narrative.

    During his life Jesus constantly warned his disciples, the demons, and those he cured not to make his identity known (the Messianic Secret). He did this because during his ministry this information would only be misunderstood. The titles, Son of God and Messiah, would only be understood during Jesus' ministry in terms of human power and glory (as we see James and John misunderstand in Mark 10:37). It is only at his death, when he is abandoned by all, even God, and he cries out to God, that Jesus can be recognized as God's Son. This is the message of Mark's Gospel. You only understand the titles, Son of God, Messiah, and king of the Jews, when you see the lowly figure executed on the cross.

77. There are three people in Jesus' passion who are not part of his inner circle (in fact, two of them are seemingly enemies of Jesus) who play central roles in ministering to Jesus, roles that should have been played by his disciples.

The woman of Bethany (14:3–9) anoints Jesus for his burial, a task that the women followers of Jesus will seek to do on the Sunday after his death, but will find Jesus' body already gone. These women followers are also asked to proclaim that Jesus is risen, but they go away afraid. Instead, it is the centurion who proclaims Jesus' true identity. Finally, his disciples (like the disciples of John the Baptist) should have buried Jesus after his death, but instead it is Joseph of Arimathea who "boldly" goes to Pilate and requests the body of the criminal Jesus. This Joseph was a distinguished member of the council (Sanhedrin), which was "looking for testimony against Jesus to put him to death" (14:55), and which "condemned him as deserving death" (14:64). It is this enemy of Jesus who is "waiting expectantly for the kingdom of God" and must have recognized its coming in the death of Jesus. It is likely that Joseph was a historical person (since he appears not only in the Synoptic Gospels but also in John) and was remembered by the community because of this important act of ministry to Jesus. In Mark's Gospel this points to the calling to serve others as you would serve Christ (see 9:41).

Section 12: Mark 16:1–20

78. By noting that the women go to the tomb to anoint Jesus and ask who will roll away the stone, Mark allows the reader to appreciate the irony. Jesus has already been anointed and the stone has been rolled away by the power of God. The women are thinking of Jesus as dead. The challenge to the disciple and reader is to recognize that Jesus is raised to life. By contrasting the plans of the women with the plan of God already worked out, Mark encourages the reader to rejoice and trust in the power and plan of God.

79. The young man is not called an angel in Mark's Gospel, but he certainly plays the role of a messenger of God.

Perhaps he is to be compared to the young man who flees naked in 14:52. The young man who flees might symbolize the disciples who flee from persecution and death, while the young man at the tomb symbolizes the disciples baptized in Christ (dressed in the baptismal garment of white) who stand at the empty tomb of Jesus and proclaim his resurrection. The one who proclaims Jesus' resurrection is not one of Jesus' inner circle, but a young man who fled naked at the arrest of Jesus. Again, Mark makes it clear that the truth about Jesus and his mission is found in the unlikeliest of places.

80. In the Gospels of Luke and John, and even in the Gospel of Matthew (which contains the same message to the disciples to go to Galilee to see Jesus), the first appearance of the risen Jesus to the disciples is in Jerusalem. In the Gospel of Mark, there is no resurrection appearance story, only a command to go to Galilee. Jesus tells his disciples to go to Galilee because that was the location of his ministry. Jesus is calling his disciples not just to experience him as the risen Lord but to follow in his footsteps now that they have experienced the whole of the Gospel story. Now they can go to Galilee and do the ministry of Jesus. Throughout the Gospel of Mark the disciples are called to follow in the way of Jesus. They are called to preach as he preaches (3:14), to heal and cast out demons as he does (6:13), to feed the crowds as he does (6:37), and to suffer and die as he did (8:34; 10:39). The command for the disciples to go to Galilee to meet Jesus is a call for them to now begin their own journey on the way of the cross.

81. According to scholars, the original ending of the Gospel of Mark was either the present verse 8 or an unknown ending that has been lost. Most likely verse 8 is the original ending of the Gospel. With this ending, Mark continues to recognize the possibility of the failure of the disciples, even after the resurrection of Jesus. After seeing the tomb empty and hearing the proclamation of the young man, the

115

women are not convinced that this is good news. In Matthew's Gospel, the one who speaks to the women at the tomb is clearly an angel. He descends from heaven and rolls back the stone from the tomb, and his appearance is like lightning. In Matthew, there is no mistaking that the message of the angel comes from God. But in Mark it is not so clear.

The good news about what God has done in Jesus and the call to follow in Jesus' footsteps is not clearly supernatural. Mark's version of the resurrection, and the good news about Jesus Christ in general, requires more faith. Mark poses a difficult and momentous challenge to the readers to make a choice. Will they trust that these words of the young man are true? Will they trust the promises made in Jesus' passion predictions? Will they trust in a God who raises from the dead? Will they go to Galilee to begin their own journey to the cross? Mark's whole Gospel has been training readers for this very difficult and life-altering choice. Mark does not make it easy.

82. The original Gospel ends with the women saying nothing to anyone. It also ends with a preposition. It seems that Mark ended his Gospel this way intentionally. What is not universally accepted is an interpretation of why Mark would end the Gospel this way. What can be said is that this ending forces the reader to reconsider all that has been said in the Gospel and to take seriously the challenge to respond. What does it mean for the disciple to go and announce to others the message of the young man that Jesus is raised from the dead? Do we believe in the power of God to raise from the dead? The unfinished nature of the Gospel challenges disciples to finish the story, to take up their crosses and follow Jesus, to preach and heal and feed and suffer and die as he did, trusting in the power of God to give life.

83. The longer ending of Mark's Gospel (16:9–20) continues Mark's theme of the failure of disciples. The disciples are

upbraided for not believing the testimony of others. In this respect, the longer ending fits with the original Gospel. In the original Gospel, the women are encouraged to believe the words of the young man. There is no apocalyptic appearance of the risen Jesus to "prove" his resurrection. There are only the words of a young man. So in the longer ending, the risen Jesus expects that his disciples will believe the words of others (16:14) and not need a resurrection appearance to have the resurrection "proved." And yet the longer ending does indicate that miraculous signs will accompany the preaching of the message of Jesus' resurrection. The signs of casting out demons, speaking in tongues, and healing the sick are less mighty deeds at the very heart of the coming of the kingdom and more simply signs that accompany the good news and that point to the message of the resurrection (16:17–18).

Bibliography

Anderson, Janice Capel, and Stephen Moore. *Mark and Method: New Approaches in Biblical Studies.* Second Edition. Minneapolis: Fortress, 2008.

Best, Ernst. *Mark: The Gospel as Story.* Edinburgh: Clark, 1983.

Collins, Adela Yarbro. *The Beginning of the Gospel: Probings of Mark in Context.* Minneapolis: Fortress, 1992.

Donahue, John. *The Gospel in Parable: Metaphor, Narrative, and Theology in the Synoptic Gospels.* Minneapolis: Fortress, 1988.

————, and Daniel Harrington. *The Gospel of Mark.* Sacra Pagina. Collegeville, MN: Liturgical Press, 2002.

Dowd, Sharyn. *Prayer, Power and the Problem of Suffering: Mark 11:22–25 in the Context of Markan Theology.* Atlanta: Scholars, 1988.

————. *Reading Mark: A Literary and Theological Commentary on the Second Gospel.* Macon, GA: Smyth & Helwys, 2000.

Flanagan, Patrick. *The Gospel of Mark Made Easy.* Mahwah, NJ: Paulist Press, 1997.

Harrington, Daniel. *What Are They Saying About Mark?* Mahwah, NJ: Paulist Press, 2005.

Juel, Donald. *The Gospel of Mark.* Interpreting Biblical Texts. Nashville: Abingdon Press, 1999.

————. *A Master of Surprise: Mark Interpreted.* Minneapolis: Fortress, 1994.

Malbon, Elizabeth Struthers. *Hearing Mark: A Listener's Guide.* Harrisburg, PA: Trinity Press International, 2002.

————. *Narrative Space and Mythic Meaning in Mark.* San Francisco: Harper & Row, 1986.

Moloney, Francis. *The Gospel of Mark.* Peabody, MA: Hendrickson, 2002.

————. *Mark: Storyteller, Interpreter, Evangelist.* Peabody, MA: Hendrickson, 2004.

Myers, Ched. *Binding the Strong Man: A Political Reading of Mark's Story of Jesus.* Maryknoll, NY: Orbis, 1988.

Rhoads, David, and Donald Mitchie. *Mark as Story: An Introduction to the Narrative of a Gospel.* Philadelphia: Fortress, 1982.

Senior, Donald. *The Passion of Jesus in the Gospel of Mark.* Collegeville, MN: Liturgical Press, 1991.